Prayeraphrases

Priceless Legacies of Prayer

*The effectual fervent prayer of
a righteous man availeth much.*
James 5:16b

*…Pray for us, that the **word** of the lord may have free course, and be **glorified**….*
2 Thessalonians 3:1

"Oh, my brethren, you will not do better than to **quote Scripture**, especially in prayer. There are no **prayers** so good as those that are full of the **Word of God**."

"O Lord Jesus, Thou art the life of my joy and the joy of my life."

— Charles H. Spurgeon

"O Lord Jesus, take my eyes and keep them fixed upon Thine everlasting beauty. Take my mouth and make it eloquent in testimony to Thy love."

— John Baillie

Prayeraphrases

Priceless Legacies of Prayer

Anthony Ruspantini

Treasure House

An Imprint of
Destiny Image® Publishers, Inc.
P.O. Box 310
Shippensburg, PA 17257-0310

"For where your treasure is,
there will your heart be also." Matthew 6:21

ISBN 1-56043-286-1

For Worldwide Distribution
Printed in the U.S.A.

This book and all other Destiny Image, Revival Press, and Treasure House books are available at Christian bookstores and distributors worldwide.

For a U.S. bookstore nearest you, call **1-800-722-6774**.
For more information on foreign distributors,
call **717-532-3040**.
Or reach us on the Internet: **http://www.reapernet.com**

Dedication

To the communion of saints—"The whole family in heaven and earth" (Eph. 3:15)—whom I love dearly and appreciate greatly.

More specifically to my wife Mary Anne, whom I love more dearly and am indebted to unspeakably!

And finally, to our children: Ellen, Carol, Anthony, and Linda who have been so supportive in this endeavor, and whom I also love dearly.

Appreciation

Let it be said that this little book would not have been possible without the grace of God working in an incredibly unique and marvelous way through the communion of the saints—I being almost inconsequential!

—The Compiler

Foreword

"Pray without ceasing," the apostle Paul wrote (1 Thess. 5:17). Many Christians find it hard to pray without *stammering*, much less pray without ceasing.

Here's a book that provides a rich resource for Christians who love prayer, as well as for those struggling in their prayer lives. Tony Ruspantini has collected in a useful format this splendid anthology of profoundly eloquent "Prayeraphrases"— expressions of praise, petition, and thanksgiving compiled from Scripture and the prayers of choice believers.

If you—like I—sometimes feel your tongue inadequate to express your thoughts in prayer, you will find reading this book a great delight. Your soul will reverberate with these phrases, and your prayer life will be greatly enriched.

This is one of those rare volumes that will become a precious companion, not something to sit on the shelf and gather dust. I commend it to you eagerly with the prayer that it will draw you before the throne of grace with even greater boldness (Heb. 4:16).

John F. MacArthur, Jr.
5 February 1993

Introduction

What Is Christ's Burning Desire for His Own?
John 17:24; 2 Corinthians 3:18 (AMP)

O that the printed word could more nearly tell forth the longing language of the heart.

Consider with me Romans 6:17 (NIV). "But thanks be to God that, though you used to be slaves to sin, you whole-heartedly obeyed the form of teaching to which you were entrusted." See also J.I. Packer's quote referring to Romans 6:17 (last quote in Appendix A). Please notice that it does not say *perfectly* obeyed, but *wholeheartedly* obeyed. O fellow Christian, I believe that if we, individually and as a Body of believers, more fully understood this marvelous verse so that it was a clear blessing to our hearts, so much so that it became a joy to explain it to others, our Christian lives would become so much simpler. Furthermore, there would be much more precious assurance of salvation in the Body of Christ than there is at this present time.

Following are a few more thoughts on assurance of salvation, and in turn, on BEHOLDING CHRIST'S GLORY and its supreme importance as a basis of earnest private prayer. Dr. D. Martyn Lloyd-Jones, in his classic work, *Studies in the Sermon on the Mount*, states, "I do not know of a better test that anyone can apply to himself or herself in this whole matter of Christian profession than a verse like this (Mt. 5:6). If this verse is to you one of the most blessed statements of the whole of Scripture you can be quite certain you are a Christian; if it is not, then you had better examine the foundations again."[1] In Thomas Brooks' outstanding book, *A Cabinet of Jewels*, he says very much the same thing. In so many words he states, and then repeats several times, words to the effect that if Psalm 119:20 was truly an accurate statement, the substance of which characterized our lives, then we were truly saved. If it did not, we were not. According to my study, Psalm 119:20 could be simply stated, "My soul continually breaks for the longing to be a knower and a doer of Thy Word, Lord."

One of the greatest and most delightful discoveries in my study of God's Word for the past 23 years has been to find the tremendous number of times the concept of longing desire and wholeheartedness is found in the Bible. Spurgeon said, "Where our longings are, there are we in the sight of God."[2] There are at least 20 different words, fairly synonymous to the word *wholehearted* that are used in Scripture. A classic case in point would be a study of the word *sound*, found in Psalm 119:80. In addition to the word "sound," the Amplified Bible also uses *sincere* and *wholehearted*. Checking the Hebrew word for "sound," #8549 in Strong's Concordance, at least 17 other English words are used to define that one Hebrew word. Included are words such as *upright*, *perfect*, and *undefiled* to name just three. Starting with the very first two verses and throughout Psalm 119, words similar to *wholehearted* are used a countless number of times.

I could associate with what Abraham Lincoln said about Matthew 5:6 and 5:8. He said that Matthew 5:6 was always one of his favorite verses while Matthew 5:8 was to him,

1.   *Studies in the Sermon on the Mount*, Vol. 1, p. 74, (Grand Rapids: Eerdmans, 1977).
2.   Treasury of David, Vol. 3, p. 212 [Psalm 119:40], (Grand Rapids: Zondervan, 1974).

most sobering. I'm sure he would have been delighted to learn that there is strong agreement that if one is characterized by Matthew 5:6, they indeed would be also characterized by Matthew 5:8. As a matter of fact, Dr. Lloyd-Jones points out that only those that mourn over their lack of purity, but have a longing desire to be pure in every way are indeed characterized as having a "pure" heart.[3] That Greek word for "pure" also means *sincere* and *wholehearted*. It is extremely significant that one of the key verses on election, Ephesians 1:4, somewhat parallels Matthew 5:8 in that "holy" means essentially "pure"; and "without blame" or "blameless" (NAS, NIV), once again carries the meaning of *sincere and wholehearted*. To summarize one more time, because the importance of this cannot be overstated, we were chosen (or elected) to be sincere and wholehearted. Thus to be characterized by sincerity and wholeheartedness for Christ and a longing desire to be pure in every way, is to be a Christian indeed! Equally as marvelous, Christ promises in John 14:21 to manifest Himself (and this certainly includes His love) to those who obey Him.

Regarding the second Biblical concept, BEHOLDING CHRIST'S GLORY, there is nothing in this world that I would rather do, and no subject I would rather talk about. More importantly, BEHOLDING CHRIST'S GLORY is without question the preeminent, foundational ingredient in prevailing private prayer. Without it there is no genuine *FERVENCY*, and as James 5:16 says, "The effectual *FERVENT* prayer of a righteous man availeth much." Psalm 39:3 reads, "While I was musing the fire burned." It essentially means that while pondering God's Word, *joy resulted*. Once again, pondering God's Word *IS* BEHOLDING CHRIST'S

---

3.   *Studies in the Sermon on the Mount*, Vol. 1, pp. 108-112, (Grand Rapids: Eerdmans, 1977).

GLORY. In trying to write about this theme however, I find myself pleading with the Holy Spirit to enable me to find the proper words which have as high a degree of clarity and brevity as possible. The two key verses would be John 17:24 and 2 Corinthians 3:18 (AMP). "Let the word of Christ dwell in you richly…" (Col. 3:16) would be the practical application very simply stated. Please permit me to bring to your attention what Spurgeon says in his quote following prayer number 100 in this compilation. Keeping that in mind, allow me to very slightly paraphrase what Spurgeon said in his sermon on John 17:24.[4] Regarding the word *will* in John 17:24, he writes, it means "forcible, distinct, resolute, determined purpose and deliberate desire." Other commentators very much agree and some add that the word "will" is equivalent to a Divine Demand! The Greek word for "will" is the strongest word for "desire" that could possibly be used! Also, because Christ prayed this matchless prayer just one day before His death, it becomes even more emphatic because it is His last will and testament! So, what is it that Christ so intensely desires us to do in John 17:24? What is the closest we can come on this earth to responding to this incredibly burning desire that Christ has for His own? Second Corinthians 3:18 (AMP) answers is perfectly.[5] "And all of us, as with unveiled face, [because *we*] *continued to behold*[6] *[in the Word of God] as in a mirror the glory of the Lord…*"

---

4.   *Metropolitan Tabernacle Pulpit*, Vol. 32, p. 174, (London: The Banner of Truth Trust, 1969).

5.   In his classic work, *The Glory of Christ*, John Owen uses 2 Corinthians 3:18 no less that eleven times to expound John 17:24 (Chicago: Moody, 1980)!

6.   The Greek word for "behold" in 2 Corinthians 3:18 also means "reflect" (see NIV).

In other words, as we read, study, memorize, retain and ponder God's Word, we are BEHOLDING Christ's Glory! This has absolutely thrilled my heart for about the last 15 years and is the very central theme of my message to God's people! What should be more impressive though, is that I genuinely believe that this is the most repeated message that the greatest preachers in the history of the Christian Church have preached to countless generations!

But how can we best **behold** or **gaze** upon Christ's glory via the Word? By pondering much the Scripture verses we have paid a real price to retain. Proverbs 4:4,21 say, "Let thine heart *retain* my words...Let them *not depart* from thine eyes; *keep them* in the midst of thine heart." If we really love God's Word as did Job (Job 23:12) and Jeremiah (Jer. 15:16), it becomes a labor of love resulting in great joy. Please notice also prayer 176 in this compilation, and hear what the Psalmist said.

I plead for your patience with me as well as responsive hearts regarding this message because I continually preach it to myself as well as tell it forth to God's people on a one-on-one basis whenever I get the opportunity. Though I approach specifics with fear and trembling, my plea to all Christians is (if you are not presently doing this), to pay any price necessary to be saturated with at least 10 or 20 verses, and, a slowly increasing number as the Holy Spirit directs. Being one of Christ's very slow learning students, I personally believe I spend at least ten hours on the average length verse over a period of 7 or 8 weeks. Some have asked if I felt it was worth spending that much time on each verse. Others have said that I would discourage people if I told them how much time I had to spend on each verse. To comment on this last statement first, I have found myself much more discouraged by those who say they can spend as brief a time as 5 minutes on each verse to have it committed to memory. I believe these people because some seem to have an uncanny ability to memorize things very fast, especially children. However, in order to truly RETAIN Scripture as Proverbs 4:4 commands, a much, much greater price has to be paid! I find that if I can finally quote a verse VERY FAST while thinking about something else, it has been learned about as well as possible. Regarding the comment about whether it is worth spending 10 hours on each verse, I have tried to respond by saying as tenderly and as sincerely as possible, in words to this effect: Even if it took 100 hours over a period of six months to retain one verse, *ISN'T JESUS WORTH IT?*

At this point, once again, I feel compelled to say that the untold hours of background reading and compilation would never have been possible without the incredibly supportive and encouraging role played by my wife, Mary Anne.

Also, I would like to express my genuine appreciation to Chuck and Donna Wetzel for the cheerful, sacrificial, and excellent workmanship that went into the typesetting of this collection. Chuck suggested the innovative title of *Prayeraphrases*. It has been very well received.

Finally, without the inspiration, encouragement and editorial advice of Phil Johnson and Dr. John MacArthur, this small book of prayers simply would not have been developed. It is the desire of both Chuck and I to relay our sentiment regarding the love we have for, and the debt of gratitude we owe to the ministry of Dr. MacArthur and Phil Johnson. It is great indeed!

Anthony J. Ruspantini

1. Come Holy Spirit, breathe light into our thoughts, life into our words. -S[1]

2. Thank You, Father, for Thy unspeakable Gift, The Lord Jesus. We know that all the unknown joys He gives were bought with agonies unknown. -S

3. How can we praise Thee enough Lord Jesus for becoming peerless in misery that we might partake of the fullness of joy. -S

4. We bow down in grateful adoration before Thee Lord Jesus; Thee who bowed so low that You might lift us up to be with Thee forever. -S

5. O Father, what are our shallow griefs compared with the infinite sorrows of Immanuel? -S

---

1. See author code listing on page 97.

6. O Thou Precious Lamb of God, Thou Monarch of the realms of misery, Thou chief among ten thousand sufferers, teach us to live beneath the shadow of Thy cross.   -S

7. Good Master, fulfill our heart's desire, and lay Thy cross on some unaccustomed shoulder even now.

-S

8. Father, prepare us for the height of blessing to which You have called us. Help us to receive gratefully the painful preliminaries necessary to fully receive Thy highest good to us.   -S

9. Thou Gentle Dove, teach us that high palaces need deep foundations, and that it takes a long time to excavate a human soul so deep that Thou art able to build a beautiful palace of grace therein.   -S

10. O Father, teach us that eminence in grace can only come by affliction.   -S

11. Thou All-Sufficient Helper, if severe trials are ordained for us, strengthen us in our infirmities and enable us to rest in Thy love.   -S

12. Help us to realize always that we are never out of the reach of Thy everlasting arms.   -S

13. Ever surround us with a sense of Thy boundless love and infinite wisdom.   -S

14. O Father, we thirst to be like Christ, to bring glory to His sacred name by complete conformity to Him. -S

15. O Father, help us to realize that "It is finished" contains an ocean of meaning in a drop of language. *[John 19:30]* -S

16. Praise Thee Our Father for the awesome stoop of Thy condescending grace, that caused You to number us among Thy redeemed ones to whom Christ spoke when He said "It is finished." *[John 19:30]* -S

17. O Our Father, Him, and then the sinner see, look through Jesus' wounds on me. *[Psalm 84:9]* -S

18. Thou Triune God, Christ's "It is finished" strikes our minds with awe and our hearts with joy because those marvelous three words, consolidated heaven, shook hell, comforted earth, delighted the Father, glorified the Son, brought down the Spirit, and confirmed the everlasting covenant to all Thine elect. *[John 19:30]* -S

19. O Thou Who only are worthy of all our love, cause us to not only know Thy precious Word, but retain it in our hearts that it might fuel the fires of our Divine affection and kindle in us lively sentiments of faith and love and rapturous joy and adoration. *[Proverbs 4:4,21; Jeremiah 15:16]* -S

20. Thrice Holy God, let our imagination extend our vision, that from this area of hallowed outlook there will arise in us rivers of gracious sympathy abundantly comforting the children of pain and grief. *[2 Corinthians 1:3-5]* -S

21. Grant us, Thou Spirit of the Living God, greater likeness to Christ by vastly extending the range of our sensitiveness to the world's sorrow and pain. *[2 Corinthians 1:3-5; Romans 12:15]* -J

22. Father, how it gladdens our hearts that Christ's actions when on earth were either the spontaneous expression of His true participation in human sorrow, or, the merciful veiling of His glory that our sense-bound eyes might see the better. *[John 11:35; Matthew 17:2; Romans 12:15]* -ML

23. O God, because the vision of Thy Divine Presence ever takes the form which our circumstances most require, we are moved to grateful praise and ardent love. *[Matthew 3:16; 17:2]* -ML

24. O Father, our constant longing desire is that through the sanctifying ministry of Thy Blessed Holy Spirit, Thine inheritance, Thy precious communion of saints, might bring continual and unspeakable joy to Thy heart. *[Ephesians 1:18]* -C

25. Eternal Father, increase our thankfulness that Thy love presides over the arrangements of grace and strikes upon the bell when the best moment has arrived; that You bless us by Thy temporary delays, as well as Thy prompt replies; that the time of the promise corresponds with the time most enriching to heart and soul. *[Psalms 37:34 (TLB)]* -S

26. God of Time and Eternity, we lack adequate words to sufficiently praise Thee that You have not only resolved

to enrich us in the future, but even now You have endowed us with the treasures of Thy love. *[1 John 1:3-4]* -S

27. Father, we praise Thee that Thy love is as certain in the night of darkness as in the brightness of the day of joy. *[Hebrews 13:5]* -S

28. O Our Father, to hear of Thy love is sweet, to believe it most precious, but to enjoy it is paradise below the skies. *[John 14:23]* -S

29. Great Triune God, we know not how to sufficiently praise Thee, that Thy love is that fountain from which all the rivers of mercy which have ever gladdened our race—all the rivers of grace in time and glory hereafter—take their rise. *[1 John 4:8; John 3:16]* -S

30. Father, may the eyes of our understanding be flooded with Divine light that we might know the hope to which we have been called and how rich is Thy glorious inheritance in Thy saints. And may this Thy glorious inheritance, consisting of Thy set-apart ones, bring unutterable joy to Thine infinite heart of love. *[Ephesians 1:18 (AMP)]* -C

31. How we praise Thee Thou Living, Loving Lord, that praying over Thy Word as Thy Holy Spirit enables us, brings great joy to our hearts as we continue to make fresh discoveries of the heights and depths, and lengths and breadths of the love of Christ and as we find new and precious meaning in texts long familiar to us. *[Ephesians 3:18-19]* -S

32. O Father, Father, at least at times may we be permitted to lose ourselves in a rapture of adoring ecstasy before Thy throne. *[1 Peter 1:8]* -S

33. Lord Jesus, we want to belong to Thee. *[Song of Solomon 2:16]* -Z

34. Father, help us to speak of Jesus in such a way that others might see at least a faint outline of His incomprehensible beauty. Then, by Thy Holy Spirit, shine through the mist of our cloudy language that Christ might be revealed in all His glory. *[Psalm 119:27,171-172]* -S

35. O, Thou Refiner, how we thank Thee that you still persevere with Thy people with settled resolve of ceaseless love till Christ be formed in us. *[Romans 8:29]* -S

36. Lord Jesus, how it thrills our hearts to think that You watch each one of Thine own as intensely as if You had not another. *[John 10:27]* -S

37. Father, how we praise Thee that although the beauty and perfections of Christ are inconceivably above our conceptions, and unutterably above our utterances, yet, somehow You are pleased to condescend to the littleness of our capacities, and enable us to experience joys unspeakable and full of glory as Christ manifests His love to us. *[1 Peter 1:8; John 14:21]* -S

38. Blessed Spirit of God, cause our faith to increase in fullness, constancy, and simplicity. *[Luke 17:5]* -S

39. Father, by Thy Spirit, grant to us a more perfect apprehension of Christ's love to us, that in turn our love to Him might be wonderfully increased. *[John 14:21]* -S

40. Grant faith to us O Lord, that is characterized by that holy expectancy that turns obstacles into helps and stones of stumbling into stepping-stones to higher things. *[Hebrews 11:11-13]* -ML

41. How we praise Thee Lord Jesus, that fellowship with Thee is the unfailing fountain of our joy. *[John 15:7,11]* -S

42. O Thou Triune Lover of Man, we are compelled to believe that Christ's Substitution for us will cause us to be overwhelmed with wonder, awe, love and praise through time and eternity. *[Psalm 84:9]* -C

43. Thou blessed Spirit of God, as often as it would glorify the Father, may the contemplation of Christ's incomprehensible Substitution for us, fill us with unutterable love to Thee and bring infinite joy to the Precious, Blessed Trinity. *[Psalm 84:9]* -C

44. O Father, Christ's Substitution in our behalf has been called the greatest marvel in the universe, the miracle of earth, the mystery of heaven, the terror of hell. Cause us to ponder it often till it works in us an intense enthusiasm of gratitude, love and praise. *[Psalm 84:9]* -S

45. O Righteous Father, we scarcely know a prayer that would better become our lips as our last prayer on

earth than—"Behold, O God our shield, and look
upon the face of Thine Anointed." *[Psalm 84:9]*   -S

46. Enable us as Thy people O our Father, to clearly quote
Thy precious promises when we are attacked by the
enemy of our souls. *[Matthew 4:4; Ephesians 6:17]*   -S

47. Father, at times allow Thy people to take venturesome
flights into the atmosphere of heaven with no other
wings but those of faith and love.   -S

48. Lord, help us to regard our lowliest, commonest
duties as the porch of the edifice of a glorious future;
to regard even the dullest moments of time as the
doorstep of celestial brilliance.   -S

49. How we praise Thee our Father, that even our most
ardent prayers only move Thy mighty arm because
The Great Mediator has stepped in to remove the sin
and ineptness of our supplication. *[John 13:8]*   -S

50. Lord Jesus, how we thank Thee that Thy dying blood
is marvelously matched by Thy living, pleading
intercessory work for Thine own. *[Hebrews 7:25]*   -S

51. Lord, the one thing we want from Thee, the thing we
seek most of all, is the privilege of meditating in Thy
temple, living in Thy presence every day of our lives,
delighting in Thy incomparable Triune perfections
and glory. *[Psalm 27:4 (TLB)]*   -C

52. O Love Immeasurable, ever expand our finite
capacity to receive Thy fullness. *[Ephesians 3:19]*   -C

53. O Thou precious Lord Jesus, take our highest manhood and saturate it with Thy Word, overflow it with Thy love. *[Psalm 119:11,97]*   -S

54. O Adorable Comforter, work in us that we might burn in our heart of hearts, while we blaze before the eyes of others. *[Philippians 2:13]*   -S

55. Father, may Thy people be the salt of the earth indeed that others may become keenly aware of the depths of their spiritual dehydration and danger.   -JFM

56. How we praise Thee, O Father, that the joys of the Holy Spirit are but the morning glances of the daylight of glory and of the sun of happiness that shall arise upon us in another world.   -TM

57. O Lord, how we praise Thee that You delight to bring Thy glory to make radiant the commonplace, that You love to fill the common waterpots with Thy mysterious wine; that You choose earthen vessels into which You pour Thy incomparable treasure.   -FM

58. Father, how we praise Thee that You are able to make a humdrum duty shine like the wayside bush that burned with fire and was not consumed, that You can make our daily business the channel of Thy grace, that You can take our disappointments and fill them with treasures of unspeakable consolation.   -J

59. O Loving Father, be pleased to use our poor, broken, stammering speech to convey the wonder of Thy grace to the weary, sinful souls of men.   -J

60. Holy Father, how we praise Thee that the very birth-hour of Christianity irradiated the seemingly insignificant doings of humble people—that when the angels went to the shepherds, common work was encircled with an immortal crown.   -FM

61. Father, how we praise Thee that the common round and daily task have a light thrown around them from the beauty of His countenance.   -FM

62. Father, if Thou be pleased to reveal to us a glint of light from among the precious truths of Thy Word, enable us to shine it forth to others.   -FM

63. Father, Father, in all worlds, in all ages, and in my little life, let the energy of Thy Will work itself out to its glorious fruition.   -FM

64. Father, may Thy Royal Will be done indeed on earth as it is in heaven!   -FM

65. Father, because we know that crises often arise in our experience when we need to know exactly what to say, we praise Thee for the Gospel mold of Thy precious Word into which we may pour the molten metal of our fervent hearts.   -FM

66. Father, may Thy Holy Spirit within us be as a fountain of Thy life and love; to work in us both to will and to do of Thy good pleasure.   -FM

67. Father, through the channels of outward expression, whether it be the written or the spoken word, help us

to be fountains of Thy Divine love and beneficent intentions toward mankind.   -FM

68. How we praise Thee Lord Jesus, that Thy disciples, humble fishermen, shone with a light which has irradiated all succeeding time.   -FM

69. Light me, O Light of Life, and let my nature henceforth have no other purpose than to shine on earth as Thou shinest in Eternal Glory, emitting a radiance of the same nature and yielding the same prism as Thine own.   -FM

70. Loving Spirit of God, be pleased to teach Thy suffering ones that joy not rooted in the soil of suffering is shallow. *[1 Peter 1:6-8]*   -J

71. Our Heavenly Father, it thrills our hearts and stretches our imagination to conceive that You delight greatly in the delight of Thy children. *[1 John 1:3-4]*   -S

72. Father, we are filled with praise to Thee for teaching us that there is a joy in life so deep that its roots are intertangled with all the roots of pain, and that there is a great gladness that shines like a rainbow against the darkest sky. *[1 Peter 1:6-8]*   -GM

73. Sweet Holy Spirit, Thou Gentle Flame, cause our love to Jesus to be so vehement and all-consuming that it might be visible in our actions, audible in our ordinary words, and even seen in our eyes in our commonest glances. *[Matthew 22:37-38]*   -S

74. O Father, may our love to Jesus be more like that of the early Christians, like a flame that fed upon the core and heart of their being; and, therefore, from its own force burned its way into the outer man, and shone there. *[Matthew 22:37-38]* -S

75. Blessed Spirit, be pleased to allow us to sense something of the amazing, immeasurable, incomprehensible love of the Father, till our very souls are inflamed with it, and our unloving nature is all on fire with love to the great Lover of the souls of men! *[John 3:16]* -S

76. O Father, enable us to esteem Holiness with apparent failure as infinitely better than success which is coupled with compromise. *[1 John 2:15]* -J

77. Lord, grant us that faith which draws energy out of splendid ideals and incorporates it in our present and immediate life. *[James 1:22]* -J

78. Cause us O Lord to earnestly desire and long after the full accomplishment of Thy glory. *[Matthew 6:9-13]*
-TM

79. Lord Jesus, long and often draw our hearts to believingly ponder Thy Divine attributes, and thus increase our faith. *[Luke 17:5]* -S

80. O Thou Living Word, how we love Psalm 119 because we could take the word of the Psalmist and lift it into one of the letters of the Apostle Paul and it

would not be dimmed by the encircling glory. *[Psalm 119]*   -J

81. Praise you, Thou Glorious Lord, for commanding the light to shine into the darkness of our hearts that we might reflect to others, the light of Thy knowledge in the face of Jesus Christ. *[2 Corinthians 4:6]*   -ML

82. Great Triune God, grant that we might see wondrous things in Thy precious Word, things that only the believing eye beholds, things that are wrapped in the invisibility of their own greatness. *[Psalm 119:18]*

-ML

83. Gracious Triune God, ever make it the magnificent obsession and passion of our lives to bring joy to Thy infinite heart of love.   -C

84. Father, enable us to realize more and more that the short-cut is seldom the finest road—that Thy round-about ways are filled with heavenly treasure—that every winding is purposed for the discovery of new wealth. O Lord, what riches we gather on the way to Thy goal.   -J

85. O Thou Blessed Master, grant us that holy reasoning of love that draws no license from grace, but rather feels the strong constraints of gratitude leading it to holiness.   -S

86. How we praise Thee Lord that You delight to hang great weights on apparently slender wires, to have

great events turn on seeming trifles, to make poverty the minister of the unsearchable riches of Christ.   -J

87. Father, grant that we might experience with wondrous spontaneity, true Christian joy as our hearts harmoniously respond to Thy continuing song of love.   -T

88. Holy Father, how we praise Thee that Thy delays are delays of love; delays according to the possibilities of restoration and recovery, or, infinitely greater blessing which Thy Divine eye discerns. *[Psalm 37:4; 37:34 (TLB)]*   -ML

89. O Lord, so excite our highest sensibilities that we might respond with instant praise and grateful love to the tender appeals of Thy precious truths.   -JP

90. May we ever O Lord, carry the glory of mighty hope into our common duty and into the cross-bearing of the dreary day. *[Romans 15:13]*   -GM

91. Lord Jesus, pour the music of Thy love through this bruised reed of Thine.   -S

92. Lord Jesus, introduce many a lost one to the Father, who will kiss them with the kisses of His love and take off their rags and clothe them with the glorious robes of Thine own righteousness.   -S

93. O Father, keep us ever mindful that we are continually writing on the pages of eternity.   -S

94. O Blessed Master, even when we pray we are often plagued with many distracting thoughts. Ever enable us to pierce them through with the incomparable sword of Thine own Spirit. *[2 Corinthians 10:5]*   -S

95. Almighty God, make us all like little children; may we look wonderingly up to heaven until the star guides us to Bethlehem; when we are there we shall not stop short of Calvary.   -JP

96. Lord, grant to us that sensitivity that we might mourn when Thou art offended and weep when Thy cause is wounded. *[Philippians 3:10]*   -S

97. Father, how we praise Thee that the first thing You do by Thy Holy Spirit is to renew the soil by the mighty enriching energies of Thy grace; then You plant the vigorous word of Thy truth and the thorns and briars of falsity are smothered in its presence. *[John 3:3; 1 Peter 1:23]*   -J

98. O God of Hope, fill all Thy people with all joy and peace in believing, that they may abound in hope through the power of Thy Blessed Holy Spirit. *[Romans 15:13]*   -C

99. Father, by faith may we see Jesus, and may His presence be so evidently realized among us that we may be filled with joy unspeakable, as if our eyes truly beheld Him in all His glory. *[John 17:24; 1 Peter 1:8]*   -S

100. How we praise Thee O Lord that it is joy to Jesus to let us behold His joy, and it is glory to us to behold

His glory and how much more so when we see Him face to face. *[John 17:24; 2 Corinthians 3:18 (AMP); Colossians 3:16]* -S

Compiler's Note: The following are Spurgeon's exact words regarding John 17:24 from *The Metropolitan Tabernacle Pulpit*, Volume 32, pg. 178:

"My text has baffled me. I am beaten back by its blaze of light. Forgive me. I had a thought, but I cannot express it. The fire of my text burns with such fervent heat that it threatens to consume me if I draw nearer to it. Easily could I step into heaven—so I feel at this moment."

101. Thou Adorable Redeemer, how indebted to Thee are we, that Thou art the Light which flames in our cold, gray mist and turns it to glory. *[John 8:12; 2 Corinthians 4:6]* -ML

102. O my Blessed Master, grant that I and all Thy people might have that clear eye that is characterized by wholeheartedness and single-minded devotion to Thee. *[Matthew 5:6; 6:22-23]* -C

103. How grateful we are to Thee our Father that the faith You give obliterates time, annihilates distance, and brings future things at once into its possession. *[Hebrews 11:8-19]* -S

104. Father, Thy smile beheld by faith gives us fullness of joy. *[Hebrews 11:5]* -S

105. Lord, enable us to escape the rut of sensual perception for the way of faith in the unseen and eternal. *[2 Corinthians 4:18]* -S

106. Father, we praise Thee that in a thousand ways, faith sweetens, enlarges and enriches life. *[Romans 5:1-5]*
-S

107. Grant us that faith, O Lord, that not only flies to heaven, but walks with Thee below. *[Romans 5:1-5]*
-S

108. O Father, may that which is written with ink in Thy Word be written with grace on our hearts. *[Psalm 119:162]* -S

109. Lord Jesus, we have need to lament that we often live in the cottage of doubt when You would be pleased to have us live in the mansion of faith. *[Hebrews 11:5-6]*
-S

110. Thou Blessed Master, grant us that oil of grace continually that keeps the flame of our faith burning. *[Luke 18:8; 17:5]* -S

111. Holy Father, grant us an oasis of faith amid this wilderness of doubt. *[Luke 18:8; 17:5]* -S

112. Lord, grant that we might be plunged into that sea of holy confidence in Thee. *[Luke 18:8; 17:5]* -S

113. Thou Redeemer and Lord, draw us so near to Thee that faith may become to us the mainspring of our lives. *[Psalm 73:28]* -S

114. Lord Jesus, rid us of fickle feeling, fill us with precious faith. *[Hebrews 11:6]* -S

115. Father, we praise Thee that the difficulties of faith are "gnats" beside the "camels" which unbelief has to swallow. *[Matthew 23:24; Hebrews 11:6]*   -ML

116. O Righteous Father, we praise Thee that the faith You give is a door through which will come all the glory that dwelt between the cherubim and will fill the secret place in our hearts.   -S

117. Lord, help us to cultivate our faith by contemplating Christ, the great Object Who kindles it; by resolving with fixed and reiterated determinations that we will exercise it. *[Hebrews 3:1; 4:11]*   -ML

118. Ever grant us O Lord that submissive faith that breeds wholehearted obedience. *[Hebrews 11:5-6]*   -C

119. Father, be pleased to give Thy people that faith that deadens us to and lifts us above the world's delights. *[1 John 5:4]*   -S

120. Lord of Love, cause our faith to be like a burning-glass, which concentrates the rays of Thy Divine Love upon our hearts and focuses them into a point that kindles our hearts into a flame and an answering, fervent love to Thee. *[1 John 4:19]*   -ML

121. Father, how we praise Thee that the holy glory of Divine communion breaks into our most commonplace circumstances and colors and transfigures them. *[1 John 1:3-4]*   -J

122. Spirit of the Living God, may Thy holy purposes lay hold of human ministries, and cause the insignificant to be glorified by the infinite. *[Isaiah 6:6-8]*   -S

123. Lord, we long to be wholehearted doers of Thy precious Word. *[Psalm 119:20]* -C

124. God of Truth, keep Thy sheep from the poisonous pastures of error. *[John 14:6; 17:17]* -S

125. Lord, make our lives to be practical transcripts of Thy Holy Will. *[Psalm 119:20]* -S

126. Gracious Father, keep us keeping Thy Royal Will. *[James 1:22; Psalm 119:20]* -S

127. Father, we praise Thee that Thy law is a storm which wrecks our hopes of self-salvation, but washes us upon the Rock of Ages. *[Galatians 3:24-25]* -S

128. Our hearts overflow with gratitude and joy when we meditate upon Thy Word which says: "Truly our fellowship *is* (not was or will be) with Thee and Thy Son the Lord Jesus." *[1 John 1:3-4]* -S

129. Father, our passionate heart's desire is that *THY* joy may be full, as the result of our fellowship with Thee. *[1 John 1:3-4]* -C

130. Father, we know that You take unutterable delight in Thy Son, and in our own baby way we delight in Him too. O Father, won't You increase our delight in Jesus, that Thy delight in Him may abound even more. *[1 John 1:3-4]* -C

131. Father, may fellowship with Thee, and Thy Son, by Thy Holy Spirit permeate the entire communion of

saints so completely, resulting in a transport so Divine, that tongue could never tell, nor lips describe the sacred rapture. *[1 John 1:3-4]*   -S

132.   O Father, what overflowing joys we experience when Thy Son manifests Himself to us. *[John 14:21]*   -S

133.   What treasure!—what gold mines!—what oceans of wealth—what mountains of sparkling gems have You conferred upon us in Christ O Our Father. *[Ephesians 2:7]*   -S

134.   O Father, the precious faith You give is the root of all our graces, the channel of communion, the weapon of prevalence, the shield of safety, the evidence of eternity and the passport of glory. Grant us O Lord, more of this inestimably precious faith. *[2 Peter 1:1-4]*
                                                                     -S

135.   Father, how we praise Thee that You have called us to be Thine own. *[Ephesians 1:4; 1 Peter 5:10]*   -C

136.   Lord, we desire to overflow with endless praise and adoration to Thee for having called us, because we know that Thy calling is but the first golden link in the endless chain of eternal mercies. *[Ephesians 1:4, 1 Peter 5:10]*   -S

137.   Sweet Holy Spirit, direct our hearts more deeply into the love of the Father and into the expectant, patient waiting for Christ. *[2 Thessalonians 3:5]*   -C

138.   O Father, we would need language celestial to speak of the sweetness of Thy love. *[2 Thessalonians 2:16-17]*
                                                                     -S

139. Father, we could weep with joy of heart that You could ever love us. *[2 Thessalonians 2:16-17]* -S

140. Triune God, with Thine infinite heart of love You love me. It is a conquering thought. It utterly overcomes me and crushes me with its weight of joy. *[2 Thessalonians 2:16-17]* -S

141. Father, how we praise Thee for the super-excellent, sublime, overcoming, triumphing greatness of Thy power. *[Ephesians 1:19]* -S

142. O the Blessedness Our Father of "being accepted in the Beloved." *[Ephesians 1:6]* -S

143. Come Holy Spirit, set our hearts on fire, express through us thunders of hallelujahs for the incomparable blessings in Christ the Father has bestowed upon us. *[Ephesians 1:3]* -S

144. Father, we know that Jesus is the brightness of Thy glory, the express image of Thy Person. How we praise Thee that Thy Deity so mildly beams through the medium of human flesh in the face of Jesus Christ. *[Hebrews 1:3; 2 Corinthians 4:6]* -S

145. Father, You have bestowed upon us the light of the knowledge of Thy glory in the face of Jesus Christ. Now it is ours, by Thy Spirit, to reflect the light, to impart the knowledge, to manifest the glory, to point to the Savior's face and to proclaim the name of Jesus Christ our Lord. *[2 Corinthians 4:6]* -S

146. Lord, it delights our hearts to see traces of the Trinity in every act of grace. *[2 Corinthians 13:14]*   -S

147. Father, help us to allow the Holy Spirit to use the truth of Thy precious Word to daily destroy sin, nourish grace, suggest noble desires and urge to holy deeds. *[John 17:17]*   -S

148. O Father how we praise Thee for the prayer of Jesus in John 17 because it rises as it proceeds like a golden ladder until it loses itself in heaven. *[John 17:24]*   -S

149. Sweet Holy Spirit, spur us on to more continual and earnest intercessory prayer and mightily strengthen our faith because we know that faith is the aqueduct along which Thy floods of mercy flow down to refresh the thirsty sons of men. *[James 5:16; Luke 17:5]*
     -S

150. O Father, as Thy unspeakable love has been shed abroad in our heart, so enable us to spread it abroad to others. *[Romans 5:5]*   -S

151. Lord, our souls break for the longing to be knowers and doers of Thy Word. *[Psalm 119:20]*   -C

152. O Father, our highest praise is inadequate to express our delight in Christ in Whom all perfections combine in perfect harmony to make Him the essence of all incomparable perfections and glory. *[Psalm 27:4 (TLB); John 17:24]*   -C

153. Lord, we freely admit that if we had the tongues of men and angels we could not worthily set forth the

glory of Christ's surpassing perfections. *[Psalm 27:4 (TLB); John 17:24]* -S

154. Blessed Savior, how we praise Thee that becoming sin for us You experienced more humiliation, darkness and agony than we could ever conceive! *[2 Corinthians 5:21]* -S

155. Father, we are eternally indebted to Thee that our condemnation has spent itself upon our gracious Representative. -S

156. Father, help us to spy Thee in the cloud and hear Thee in the thunder. *[1 John 3:1]* -S

157. O Father, may love to Thee and the Lord Jesus and Thy Blessed Holy Spirit be the overriding characteristic of our lives. *[1 John 3:1; Matthew 22:36-37]* -S

158. Lord Jesus, we praise Thee that trials bring us to Thy feet. -S

159. We adore Thee O Our Father that trials not only lay us low and keep us there, but give new life to prayer. *[1 Peter 1:6-7]* -S

160. O Father, be pleased to kindle enthusiasm of spirit and burning zeal in the hearts of Thine own. *[Revelation 3:19]* -S

161. Holy Spirit, grant us that tongue of zeal that speaks with matchless might. *[Revelation 3:19]* -S

162. Lord Jesus, draw us nearer and nearer to Thyself in ever growing fellowship of affection. *[John 15:9]* -S

163. Thou Husband of our souls, how we praise Thee that You overflow with Divine affection to us everyday and all the day. *[John 15:9]* -S

164. How we praise Thee Our Father, that in the ocean of Jesus' love to us, there is neither shore nor bottom. *[John 15:9]* -S

165. Thou Triune God, we overflow with praise to Thee for Thy unsought favors of unspeakable love. -S

166. We thank Thee Lord for Thy perpetual mercies of unslumbering grace. *[Ephesians 2:7]* -S

167. Spirit of God, help us to read more clearly the heart of Jesus. Help us to dive more deeply into the meaning of what He has done for us. *[Hebrews 3:1; 12:1-2]* -S

168. Lord Jesus, sensitize the hearts of all Thine own, that Thy image might be more clearly seen in us. *[2 Corinthians 3:18 (AMP)]* -C

169. Father, how we praise Thee for Him whose head, once crowned with thorns, is now radiant with the diadem of universal dominion. *[Hebrews 12:1-2]* -S

170. Spirit of the Living God, we praise Thee that Thy Word to us is overflowingly alive. *[Hebrews 4:12]* -S

171. Lord Jesus, how grateful we are that Thy Word not only casts down the strongholds of doubt but cuts off the head of giant despair. *[Hebrews 4:12]* -S

172. God of Sovereign Grace, how grateful we are to Thee, that in Thy fathomless, boundless love to us, You carry every chosen vessel of mercy from grace to glory. -S

173. Holy Spirit, create in us a strong passionate desire to accept and obey God's Word in everything, and to be conformed to it in thought and life. Then Blessed Spirit, may that passionate desire ultimately get the victory. *[Psalm 119:20]* -S

174. Father, as Thy people, empower us by Thy Spirit to remain tenaciously clinging to Jesus, livingly knit to Him. *[John 15:7]* -S

175. Thou Living Word, help us to be more believingly familiar with the promises in Thy written Word. -S

176. Nothing is perfect except Your Words. O how I love them. I think about them all day long. *[Psalm 119:96-97 (TLB)]* -C

177. Lord we thank Thee that at times, truth reserves her rarest beauties for the moment when she is being shared. *[John 17:17]* -J

178. Sweet Spirit, teach us that the price of retention is expression. *[Proverbs 4:4,21]* -J

179. Father, we praise Thee that the glory You reveal to us in Christ is like solar light falling upon infirm eyes in rays of softest shining. *[Hebrews 1:3]* -J

180. God of Truth, we are grateful that You have taught us that the full glory of truth only breaks upon us when we proclaim it. *[Psalm 119:27]* -J

181. Lord, You fill us with wonderment at times when in the moment of communication, truth reveals an unexpected wealth. *[Psalm 119:9-16]* -J

182. Lord Jesus, surprise us often with unexpected manifestations of Thy love. *[John 14:21]* -J

183. We praise Thee Lord that truth is vivified in the very ministry of expression. *[Psalm 119:27]* -J

184. Lord, open the doors and windows of our soul to the Sun of Righteousness. *[Psalm 84:11]* -S

185. Father, grant us that faith that rests so absolutely and confidingly on Thee that Thy bare Word becomes to us the infallible source of certitude with regard to all the shifting hours of time, and, to the steadfast day of an eternity whose change is blessed growth to an unreached and undeclining noon. *[Hebrews 11:6]* -ML

186. O to be borne along by the irresistible force of eternal love! -S

187. Ah Lord Jesus, Thou hast assured me of Thy love by Thy wounds. O that I loved Thee better in return! *[John 15:9]* -S

188. O Lord Jesus, eternity will be too short to adequately praise Thee for Thy incomprehensible condescension

in descending from highest heaven to become the Man of Sorrows for our sakes! -S

189. O Father, at times we sense a desperate need to see dramatic manifestations of Thy mercies. *[Ephesians 2:4]* -C

190. Lord Jesus, we find our bliss repeated in the joy of all whom You love as You love us. -S

191. Father, when we pray, enable us to accurately quote Thine own Words in the power of Thy blessed Holy Spirit. *[1 John 5:14-15]* -C

192. Thou prayer hearing God, allow us to believingly remember what You have promised in Thy Word, and then permit us to remind Thee that You promised it. *[Psalm 119:49]* -S

193. Thou Triune God, how wondrous! how marvelous that in prayer we should be able, as it were, to move the arm that moves the stars, and hold the King who holds the waters in the hollow of His hand! *[Psalm 119:49]* -S

194. Spirit of the living God, enable us to plead mightily by presenting before the Father His own sacred Word! *[Psalm 119:49]* -S

195. Oh that we had the power to grasp Thy Word as it ought to be grasped! *[Psalm 119:49]* -S

196. Oh for the grace to plead the promise and rest upon it! *[Psalm 119:49]* -S

197. How we praise Thee our Father that You choose us for Thy love, and You love us because You have chosen us. *[Psalm 119:49]*   -S

198. Eternal Father, O that we might be people of prayer, because we know that true prayer is the shadow of a coming blessing. *[Psalm 119:49]*   -ML

199. Because we know Our Father, the higher up the mountain the more boisterous the winds; we praise Thee even amid our afflictions. *[Psalm 119:50]*   -S

200. Father, may we experience the fire, if only thus we can realize Thy divine presence. *[Psalm 119:50]*   -S

201. Holy Spirit, enable us to ever bring with us Thy precious Word, brimming with rich promises, because like the Psalmist we have found that it is our comfort in our affliction. *[Psalm 119:50]*   -S

202. O Father how we praise Thee that even the gates of despair shall open with that key called Promise, found in Thy precious Word! *[Psalm 119:50]*   -S

203. Lord, we know that we must be cut with the sharp knife of affliction, for only then can You make use of us. *[Psalm 119:50]*   -S

204. Lord Jesus, how we praise Thee that You came to earth to bring us truth steeped in love, truth saturated with mercy. *[John 1:14,17]*   -S

205. O Father we praise Thee for Jesus because we know that His grace is all true, and His truth is all gracious. *[John 1:14,17]*   -S

206. Almighty Father, how shall we, who are but as a twinkling dewdrop on a blade of grass, reflect the glory of the Sun of Righteousness? *[John 1:14,17]* -S

207. Father, it staggers our imagination, that because of Thy miracle of love, insignificant creatures such as we should ever be one with Incarnate Deity, and so much so that we will never be separated throughout the ages. *[John 1:14,17]* -S

208. O Thou morning and evening Lamb, we praise Thee everlastingly that Thy Gospel is a wonderful embodiment of omnipotent wisdom, grace and truth. *[John 1:14,17]* -S

209. Blessed Lord Jesus, we praise Thee that You are not only our Priest to put away our sin, but Prophet to remove our ignorance, and King to subdue our wandering hearts. -S

210. Thou Son of God, Thou Savior of men, Thou art very God of very God and our longing desire is to give ourselves more fully to Thee. *[John 1:1,14]* -C

211. Grant us that faith that wholeheartedly obeys for very love of Thee. *[Galatians 5:6]* -C

212. O how we desire to please Thee Lord! *[Psalm 119:20; Matthew 5:6]* -C

213. O what a bracelet of mercies they will make when all the days of our lives are threaded on time's string! *[Ephesians 2:4]* -S

214. Oh God, shall saints be shams when sinners are so real? *[Matthew 3:8; 7:16]* -S

215. We praise Thee Our Father, that miracles of grace have been wrought in us more numerous than grains of sand on the sea-shore. *[Ephesians 2:4]* -S

216. Father, we rejoice that Thy hand has been laid upon the canvas of our lives which is matchless even in its outlines, and foundation colors; and that You have never yet thrown away a canvas upon which You have once commenced a masterpiece. *[Ephesians 2:10]* -S

217. O Loving Father, may the meekness, uprightness, truth and purity of Jesus shine through our lives for all men to see. *[Matthew 5:16]* -S

218. Father, we praise Thee for that mystic union between Christ and Thine own which shall never be dissolved through endless ages of eternity. *[John 17:23]* -S

219. O to be well-pleasing in Thy sight Our Father! *[Ephesians 2:10]* -C

220. Father, help all who name the name of Christ to soberly ponder that there is no ordination to salvation apart from sanctification. *[Ephesians 2:10]* -S

221. Lord, may the path of Thy set-apart ones be luminous with holiness. *[Proverbs 4:18; Ephesians 2:10]* -S

222. Blessed Trinity, grant that we might joyfully believe that You have decreed the holy lives of Thy people as

much as You have decreed our ultimate glorification with Thee in Heaven! *[Romans 8:30; Ephesians 2:10]*   -S

223.   Lord Jesus, we praise Thee for Thy condescending love which made Thee willing to exchange the supernal joys of heaven for the jeers of earth. *[John 1:14]*   -S

224.   Precious Spirit of God, it is our heart's desire to live our lives in every aspect fully under Thy Divine influence! *[Ephesians 5:18; Colossians 3:16]*   -C

225.   Father, may we who have believed in Jesus be transformed altogether by Thy Blessed Holy Spirit that great joy might be brought to Thy heart! *[2 Corinthians 3:18 (AMP)]*   -C

226.   Lord, grant that we might enter more thoroughly into the secret place of the Most High and more constantly abide under the shadow of the Almighty. *[Psalm 91:1,4]*   -C

227.   Father we praise Thee that we have had communion with Christ, but we long for closer communion yet. *[1 John 1:3-4]*   -S

228.   Father, may we never rest satisfied feeding on crumbs when You have created us to feed abundantly on the Bread of Heaven! *[John 6:54]*   -S

229.   Lord, we praise Thee that You are eminent in overruling all opposition to Thy cause. *[1 Corinthians 16:9]*   -S

230. Father, we praise Thee that in Thy Sovereignty even the most crafty and cruel enemy becomes the unwilling agent of bringing greater glory to Thee. *[1 Corinthians 16:9]* -S

231. We can never thank Thee enough O Lord for Thy precious Word, a single word of which at times opens up infinite horizons to our souls. *[Jeremiah 15:16]* -S

232. Thou Living Word, our highest earthly enjoyments are but a shadow in comparison to the joy that floods our hearts when we ponder Thy incomparable Word! *[Jeremiah 15:16; Psalm 39:3]* -S

233. Thank You Lord Jesus that Thy Word is always fresh and marvelously in tune with the ever changing needs of our daily lives. *[Psalm 119:96-97 (TLB)]* -S

234. Father, we praise Thee that Thy Book contains not only utterance for our deepest griefs, but songs for our supernal joys. *[Jeremiah 15:16]* -S

235. Sweet Spirit of Truth, we praise Thee that Thy precious Gospel not only commands holiness, but it produces it. *[Hebrews 12:14]* -S

236. Oh to swim in love, upborne by grace! *[John 15:9]* -S

237. Oh to throw one's self into the might and majesty of God! *[Ephesians 1:19]* -S

238. Oh to plunge into the Godhead's deepest sea! *[2 Corinthians 13:14]* -S

239. Continually create in us Sweet Holy Spirit an insatiable craving to go deeper into the Triune Love of God! *[2 Corinthians 13:14]* -S

240. Oh to at times experience the heavenly delirium of burning zeal in Thy service, Thou Divine Master! *[Philippians 3:13-14]* -S

241. What a blessing it is that failing, flagging, fainting spirits, by waiting upon Thee Lord, shall renew their strength. *[Isaiah 40:31]* -S

242. Oh Our Father, cause us to come to Thee daily with high expectations, because we know that You will not disappoint them. *[Ephesians 3:20]* -JP

243. We praise Thee Lord that Thy powerful Word rules in the lives of Thine elect. *[Hebrews 4:12]* -S

244. We praise Thee Thou Triune God for Thy infinite power and Thy infinite Love, and Thy infinite Love and Thy infinite power! *[Revelation 19:6; 1 John 4:8]*

-C

245. "Filled with all the fullness of God"— Oh, God, be it ours by sweet experience to ascend that staircase of supernal light! *[Ephesians 3:14-19]* -S

246. Sweet Holy Spirit, vastly enlarge our faith and strengthen us in every necessary way to live in the atmosphere of this unspeakably marvelous prayer! *[Ephesians 3:14-21]* -C

247. Spirit of the Living God, enable us, as much as it would be possible in the flesh, to behold Christ's glory in the most perpetual, unclouded way, thus fulfilling Jesus' hearts' desire. *[John 17:24; 2 Corinthians 3:18 (AMP)]* -C

248. Lord Jesus, how can we express adequately our love to Thee for descending from the highest realms of glory to the cross of deepest woe. *[John 17:5; 19:30]* -S

249. Our supreme desire, the thing we seek most of all, is to bring Triune glory to Thee Thou Triune God! -C

250. Grant us O Lord that spiritual discipline that frees us from the gravity of this present age and allows us to soar with angels and saints triumphant. *[Philippians 2:12-13]* -S

251. Help us Thou Spirit of God to, with regularity, enter Thy gymnasium of Divine discipline. *[Philippians 2:12-13]* -C

252. Oh Righteous Father, enable our spiritual eyes to clearly see the shattering results of straying from Thy Holy Word. *[Romans 6:22]* -C

253. Father, save us from idleness, that horrible sin that caused King David's devastating decline. *[Numbers 32:20-23]* -C

254. Father, grant to each of us as Thy children, the discipline of Divine awareness to a supreme degree! *[Philippians 4:5]* -S

255. Lord, help us to clearly perceive that faith is the basis of effort, and effort is the crown of faith. *[Philippians 2:12-13]* -S

256. Father, we praise Thee for the wondrous transfiguring effect resulting from the thought of Thy will continually brought into connection with the smallest of the deeds which circumstances, relationships, occupations and the like constitute our duties. *[Matthew 6:10]* -S

257. Lord Jesus, the sight of Thee to our inward eye is the bliss of solitude, and ministers strength to our life in solitude or in society. *[Hebrews 3:1; 12:1]* -ML

258. Lord, teach us that the eye that is focused to look at things on the earth cannot see the stars. *[Hebrews 3:1; 12:1]* -ML

259. Thank You Father that we are children of the day, and our dreams are one day to pass into the sober certainty of waking bliss. *[1 Thessalonians 5:5-6]* -ML

260. Lord, help us to distinguish fleeting trivialities from eternal realities. *[1 John 2:15]* -ML

261. Grant us O Lord a deliberate preference to things unseen and eternal. *[2 Corinthians 4:18]* -ML

262. Father, grant us that faith that clearly reveals the things promised and knits us so closely to them that

we cannot help but feel a blessed separation from the things that are round about us. *[2 Corinthians 4:18]*

-ML

263. Lord, teach us that no soul can look so as to behold unseen glories if its eye be turned to all these vanities here. *[2 Corinthians 4:18; Psalm 119:37]* -ML

264. Enable us O Lord to cultivate the faculty of beholding, and to train the eye to look into that telescope that pries into distant worlds, and brings eternal glories near. *[Hebrews 11:26-27]* -ML

265. Cause us to realize Lord, that the vision of faith is far more correspondent to the realities, and far more satisfying to the eye that gazes, than is any vision of the sight of sense. *[2 Corinthians 4:18]* -ML

266. Father we praise Thee that in Christ Thy character is bloomed forth to the eyes of faith. *[John 1:1,14]* -J

267. Thou Triune God, in Christ we see Thy majesty issuing in grace. *[John 1:16-17]* -J

268. How grateful we are Our Father, that in Christ we see Thy glory falling upon our infirm eyes in rays of softest shining. *[John 1:16-17]* -J

269. Holy Spirit, we praise Thee that the sight that faith gives is, solid, substantial, clear and certain. *[2 Corinthians 5:7]* -ML

270. Lord, may the clear vision of that permanent future detach us from the perishable present. *[Hebrews 11:26-27]*   -ML

271. Father, let us polish the lenses of our telescopes, and use them not only for distances on earth's low levels, but to bring eternal glories near. *[2 Corinthians 4:18]*

-ML

272. Father, our gratitude to Thee is boundless because in Christ we see Thy holiness consummated in tenderness. *[John 1:1,14]*   -J

273. Praise Thee O Lord Jesus that in Thee we see truth in the radiant robes of mercy. *[John 14:6]*   -J

274. Praise Thee Lord Jesus that in Thee we see the splendor of the Godhead shedding itself abroad in the delicacy of love. *[Colossians 2:9]*   -J

275. Praise Thee Lord Jesus that in Thee we see the manifested presence of the Triune God, warm and gentle as sunshine, clean and pure as fire! *[Colossians 2:9]*   -J

276. Lord, teach us that time is only redeemed from triviality when it is seen to be the preparation for eternity, and that earth is never so fair as when we discern and use it as the vestibule of heaven. *[Ephesians 5:16]*   -ML

277. Spirit of God, cause us to soberly ponder upon the very real possibility that trifles an inch from our eyes

are big enough to shut out heaven and all its stars.
[2 Corinthians 4:18]   -ML

278.   As we trust in Thee and Thy infallible Word Blessed
       Spirit, may the future, so dim and uncertain to
       unaided eyes, become as certain to us as the past, and
       expectation as reliable as memory. *[Hebrews 11:7]*
                                                           -ML

279.   Lord Jesus, grant us continuous, calm communion
       with Thee and be our constant companion whether in
       solitude or in a crowd. *[Hebrews 11:5-6]*   -ML

280.   Lord Jesus, may our lives be characterized by
       whole-hearted, continuous, persevering seeking of
       Thee. *[Hebrews 11:5-6]*   -C

281.   Sweet Holy Spirit, keep our thoughts and our love
       directed towards Jesus, even among the trivialities
       and commonplace duties of life. *[Hebrews 12:1]*   -GM

282.   Thou interceding Christ, apply to our hearts and lives
       all the merit You obtained by Thy incomprehensible
       suffering and death for us upon the cross. *[Hebrews
       7:25]*   -S?

283.   Lord Jesus, let us not lose sight of the fact that You
       came into the world to bring peace at the far end, but
       righteousness at the near end, and therefore strife.
       [Hebrews 7:2]   -ML

284.   We praise Thee Sweet Holy Spirit for first imputing
       the very righteousness of Christ to our hearts and

lives, and then giving us the sweet assurance of peace with the Father. *[Hebrews 7:2; 2 Corinthians 5:21]*   -S

285. Holy Spirit, help us to work out our own salvation in fear and trembling with the intensest efforts since it is You who work in us both to will and to do of Thine own good pleasure. *[Philippians 2:12-13]*   -C

286. We praise Thee, Thou Blessed Redeemer, for taking verses that have been familiar to us for years and applying them to our hearts and lives with expanded and undreamed of fullness. *[Luke 24:32]*   -S

287. Father, may the holy glory of Divine communion with Thee, often break into our most commonplace circumstances and color and transfigure them. *[1 John 1:3-4]*   -J

288. Sweet Holy Spirit, let us meditate and gaze and worship, until He, who is the outshining of Divine glory, shines into our very hearts that we might reflect that Divine glory to others. *[2 Corinthians 3:18 (AMP); 4:6]*   -AM

289. Lord, give us as much of Thy strength, as much of Thy love, as much of Thy righteousness, as much of Thyself as it is possible for creatures in union with the Son of Thy love to possess. *[Ephesians 3:19]*   -MR

290. Lord Jesus, we praise Thee, that of all other places, the redeemed soul was especially created for a shrine in which may shine forth Thy Divine glory. *[2 Corinthians 4:6]*   -GB

291. We praise Thee, Our Father, that man is a many faceted diamond to catch and reflect back the glory of Thine only Son. *[2 Corinthians 4:6]*   -T

292. We praise Thee Our Father that Thy highest glory is the exhibition of forgiving and long-suffering love. *[1 John 4:8]*   -ML

293. Thank You Lord Jesus, for condescending to the companionship of our grief that You might lift us up into a share of Thy glory. *[Hebrews 2:10]*   -ML

294. We praise Thee Our Father, that You have an absolutely, unbelievable ability, in an economy of words, to say an eternity of truth. *[John 19:30]*   -JFM

295. Grant that we should rejoice and profit much from all the faithful leaders You send us, Lord. *[1 Corinthians 3:22-23]*   -JFM

296. Father, our earnest prayer is that by Thy Holy Spirit, You would create in many of Thy people today, a genuine hunger and thirst for the very best books among the vast variety that are available at this time. *[2 Timothy 4:13]*   -C

297. Father, may we sit more humbly and with diligent attention at the feet of the masters, those Pastor-Teachers and others whom Thy Blessed Holy Spirit has hand picked for our incredible benefit. *[Ephesians 4:11-14]*   -C

298. We are pleased Our Father, that You see fit to let the truth sift down to us through the prism of many minds. *[Ephesians 4:11-14]*   -WB

299. Father, as the communion of saints is in our Creed, so may we benefit by them in our lives! *[Ephesians 3:17-19; 4:11-14]* -TW

300. Praise Thee, O Lord, for often surprising us with many manifestations of Thy love and goodness to us. -C

301. Lord, open our eyes to see wonderful things in Thy Word. We are but pilgrims here on earth: how we need a map—and Your commands serve as our chart and guide. *[Psalm 119:18-19 (TLB)]* -C

302. Reassure us sweet Holy Spirit, that Thy promises are truly for us! *[Psalm 119:38 (TLB)]* -C

303. Holy Spirit, help us to immovably cling to the Lord Jesus, the immovable Rock of our salvation. *[Psalm 95:1]* -C

304. We praise Thee our Father that Thy many promises all find their Yes answer in Him. For this reason we also utter the Amen to Thee through Him, in hopes that You, Our Father, might receive much glory! *[2 Corinthians 1:20 (AMP)]* -FM

305. Father, ever lift us above the selfish and cowardly dependence on externals and surroundings, men and things, on which we are all tempted to live. *[2 Corinthians 4:18]* -MG

306. Teach us O Lord, that the highest gifts of Thy grace and the greatest truths of Thy Word are meant to

regulate even the tiniest things in our daily lives. *[Colossians 3:23-24]* -MG

307. Our Father, grant us a wholesome disregard of externals, and a hearty dependence upon Thee! *[2 Corinthians 4:18]* -MG

308. Lord, help us to be like a tree, rooted deep, and therefore rising high in praise to Thee. *[Ephesians 3:17]* -ML

309. Lord Jesus, abundantly supply us with recipient love, corresponding to the longing desire of Thy infinite heart, to lavish Thy love upon us. *[1 John 3:1; John 13:1]* -ML

310. Father, may our upward glance of aspiration and petition, and necessity, correspond to Thy downward glance of Thy love bestowing itself upon us. *[1 John 3:1; 2 Corinthians 4:18]* -ML

311. Thou Triune God, be Thou my will, my Emperor, my Commander, my All! -ML

312. Father, may our lives be characterized by contemplating and reflecting Christ. *[2 Corinthians 3:18 (AMP)]* -ML

313. O Father, may our souls be like mirrors, which at once behold and reflect the glory of Christ. *[2 Corinthians 3:18 (AMP)]* -ML

314. We praise Thee Lord Jesus, that You are the light that reveals itself to us by striking with quickening

impulse on the eye of our spirits when we behold Thee by faith. *[2 Corinthians 3:18 (AMP)]* -ML

315. Father, help us to soberly realize, that we are only clear from the blood of men when we, for our parts, make sure that if any light be hid, it is hid not by reason of obscurity or silence on our parts, but only by reason of the blind eyes, before which the full-orbed radiance gleams in vain. *[2 Corinthians 3:18 (AMP)]*

-ML

316. By Thy Holy Spirit O Our Father, grant to us that gaze of love and trust that molds us by silent sympathy into the likeness of His wondrous beauty. *[2 Corinthians 3:18 (AMP)]* -ML

317. Sweet Holy Spirit, enable us to see to it that we neither turn away our gaze, nor relax our efforts till all that we have beheld in Him is repeated in us! *[2 Corinthians 3:18 (AMP)]* -ML

318. Loving Lord, teach us to learn that in order to get the highest good out of things that are seen, we must bring into the field of vision things unseen and eternal. *[2 Corinthians 4:18]* -ML

319. Lord, may we be among those who look out into the eternities and thus have the true measuring rod and standard by which to estimate the true importance and necessity of the things that are present. *[2 Corinthians 4:18]* -ML

320. Father, teach us that there is nothing that so lifts the commonplace into the solemn, and invests with

everlasting and tremendous importance everything we do here, as seeing all things in the light of eternity. *[2 Corinthians 4:18]* -ML

321. Lord, help us to perform our duties each day with the light of the eternal world full upon them. *[2 Corinthians 4:18]* -ML

322. Father, we know that to look at things unseen and eternal is only possible through Jesus Christ. We know that He is the only window which opens out and gives the vision of that far-off land. *[2 Corinthians 4:18]* -ML

323. Sweet Holy Spirit, grant us that concentrated attention and steadfast look needed to make the invisible visible! *[2 Corinthians 4:18]* -ML

324. We praise Thee Thou Holy Spirit of God, that the very desires You create in us are themselves confirmations of their own fulfillment. *[2 Corinthians 5:5 (AMP)]* -ML

325. Our desires are the prophesies of His gifts. *[Psalm 37:4]* -ML

326. Father, help us to please Him "who pleased not Himself." *[Romans 15:3]* -ML

327. Holy Spirit, help us to be ever gazing with the believing eyes of our hearts upon that which kindles our love to Him. *[Hebrews 12:1]* -ML

328. We praise Thee Lord Jesus that Thy yoke is easy, not because it is lighter, but because it is padded with love. *[Matthew 11:30]* -ML

329. Lord Jesus, may the power of Thy echoed love rule our lives! *[2 Corinthians 5:14]* -ML

330. O Thou tender, loving Creator, how can we even begin to comprehend Thy infinite longing for our love and Thy infinite desire for unity between Thee and us? *[Matthew 22:37; John 17:23-26]* -S?

331. O Lord Jesus, help us to contemplate often Thy tears of imploring love! *[2 Corinthians 5:20; Matthew 23:37]*
-S

332. Father, may we never be found shutting our ears against the tender, imploring love of Christ. *[2 Corinthians 5:20]* -S

333. Oh, that these lips had language, or that these hearts could speak without them! Then would we plead with every soul within this place, and plead as for our very lives, that you would receive the love Christ offers you, and be reconciled to God! *[2 Corinthians 5:20 (TLB)]* -S

334. Triune God, how can we begin to conceive Thy beseeching urgency and intensity of Divine desire to save and manifest Thy love to Thy creatures? *[2 Corinthians 5:20 (TLB)]* -C

335. Father, may our Christian liberality spring spontaneously from the conscious possession of Christ's riches. *[2 Corinthians 8:1-12]* -S?

336. Father, teach us that when willingness to give is embodied in the largest gift possible, even trifles have a place in Thy storehouse of precious things. *[2 Corinthians 8:1-12; Mark 12:42-44]* -S

337. We praise Thee Lord Jesus, that self-impartation was the underlying theme of all Thy precious life from Bethlehem to Calvary. *[2 Corinthians 8:9]* -S

338. Lord Jesus, teach us that it is only as we abide in Thee, and Thy Words abide in us that You are able to communicate Thy love to unworthy and transgressing recipients such as us. *[John 15:7,11]* -ML

339. Blessed Redeemer, as You stooped to earth, veiling the Divine with the human, so may we rise to heaven, clothing the human with the Divine. *[2 Corinthians 8:9]* -ML

340. We praise Thee Lord Jesus for becoming like unto us, that each of us may become like unto Thee. *[2 Corinthians 8:9]* -S

341. Blessed Savior, how we thank Thee that You shared our human poverty that we may share Thy Divine riches! *[2 Corinthians 8:9]* -ML

342. How we praise Thee Lord Jesus, that we can take Thee as the pattern of our conduct as well as the object of our trust. *[1 John 2:6]* -ML

343. Father, teach us that we too must learn to stoop to forgive, to impart ourselves, and must die by

self-surrender and sacrifice, if we are ever to communicate any life or good to others. *[2 Corinthians 8:9]* -ML

344. May the tree of our life's doings grow to Thy glory. *[2 Corinthians 8:11]* -ML

345. Oh Lord, who can ever speak adequately and in full correspondence with reality regarding what it is to have God's pardoning love flowing in upon our souls? *[2 Corinthians 9:15]* -ML

346. Thou Unspeakable Gift, how we praise Thee that throughout eternity there will be endless growth in the appropriation of Thee! *[2 Corinthians 9:15]* -ML

347. Teach us Sweet Spirit that we will best appreciate the simplicity of the Gospel when we have most honestly endeavored to fathom its depths. *[2 Corinthians 9:15]*
-ML

348. Lord Jesus, cause our love to Thee to be so ardent that our hearts will be kept clear from all competing affections. *[Luke 14:26]* -S

349. Grant us O Lord that single-mindedness that longs to obey Thee swiftly, cheerfully, and constantly! *[Matthew 22:37]* -ML

350. O Thou Blessed Master, we long to be characterized by unhesitating, unfaltering, unreserved, and unreluctant obedience to Thy every wish. *[Matthew 22:37]* -WS

351. Praise Thee, Lord Jesus, that Your strength loves to work in our conscious weakness when it passes into conscious dependence. *[2 Corinthians 12:8-9]* -ML

352. Teach us Sweet Spirit that the secret of all noble, heroic, useful, happy living lies in the paradox, "When I am weak, then am I strong!" *[2 Corinthians 12:8-9]* -ML

353. Lord Jesus, we praise Thee that Thy cross is not only the ground of our hope, but the pattern of our conduct. *[Galatians 6:14]* -ML

354. O Thou Captain of our salvation, save us from corruption caused by selfish and inglorious ease. *[Ephesians 5:16]* -ML

355. Lord, we might as truly say, "Our Father, Thou art our heaven." *[1 John 2:13]* -S

356. Come to me my Father; manifest Thyself to me, for I cannot live without Thee. *[John 14:23]* -S

357. Thou Lover of the souls of men, ever keep our hearts aglow with gratitude to Thee! *[1 Thessalonians 5:18]* -S

358. Thy love O God is a shoreless ocean into which we may be baptized, and out of which we may be filled until we overflow. *[1 John 4:10]* -ML

359. Sweet Holy Spirit, because Jesus is our Beloved, how it assures out hearts that we are accepted in the Beloved. *[Ephesians 1:6]* -S

360. Father, by Thy Holy Spirit, enable us to feed much upon Christ via the Word, till we are enveloped by His love and overflowing with His joy. *[John 15:7,11]*
-C

361. Lord, cause those sublime truths concerning things unseen and eternal to become more and more precious to our hearts. *[2 Corinthians 4:18]*   -S?

362. Father, we would see Jesus more from Thy point of view, and thereby worship and please Thee more and serve Thee better. *[John 12:21]*   -S?

363. Oh, Peace of God, rule Thou me. *[Colossians 3:15]*   -S

364. We praise Thee O Father that the bodily resurrection of Christ is the most indisputably established historic fact in the annals of human existence! *[Acts 1:3]*   -E

365. Blessed Spirit of the Living God, let nothing and no one ever shake the faith of Thy people in the glorious resurrection of Christ! *[Acts 1:3]*   -S

366. We praise Thee Lord that though we are as the moon, shining by reflected light, yet Jesus loves the moonlight of our love and rejoices in it. *[John 17:26]*
-S

367. Let us shine on Christ with all the light we can possibly reflect of the Father's love. *[John 17:26]*   -S

368. Oh Blessed Holy Spirit, teach us all we are able to learn of the Father's love to His Son, or else we will

not love the Father as we should for the amazing sacrifice which He made in giving Jesus to us. *[John 17:26]*   -S

369. Oh wondrous thought Our Father, that Thine own love to Jesus should dwell in our hearts! *[John 17:26]*
                                                                        -S

370. Spirit of Holiness, may the flame of love within our hearts be continually revived by the fuel of holy knowledge which You place upon it via Thy infallible Word of Truth! *[John 17:17]*   -S

371. Father, grant that each and every one of Thy Children might be by love compelled to praise Thee endlessly for such a prayer as this! A prayer so living, so earnest, so loving, so Divine, deserves the most diligent study and meditation by all believers. Grant that it may be so Lord! *[John 17]*   -S

372. Thou Blessed Spirit of God, cause us as Thy people to be wonderfully self forgetful as we become more and more enraptured by the beauty and glory of Christ! *[John 17:5,24]*   -C

373. Triune God, instill in Thy people a deeper sense of wonder and awe, adoration and worship, as we more keenly perceive Thy presence among us. *[2 Corinthians 13:14]*   -S?

374. Oh God, our supreme desire is that Thy will be done not only in our lives but in Thy entire universe! *[Matthew 6:10]*   -C

375. Father, marvelously multiply our gratitude to Thee as we ponder with incomprehensible joy that we have been chosen in eternity to be Thine own. *[Ephesians 1:4]* -LJ

376. O Father, because we have been saved in eternity, cause us to persevere with great intensity and zeal for the advancement of Thy Kingdom. *[Ephesians 1:4; Matthew 6:10]* -LJ

377. Grant to us a restful realization of Thy gracious and almighty presence, Thou Eternal God. *[Hebrews 11:6]*
-J

378. Father, we praise Thee for the Spirit-filled utterances of Thy communion of saints. How thankful we are that we are permitted to share in the fruits of their painful toil! *[Ephesians 3:17-19]* -J

379. We praise Thee our Father for the hope You give to us that the dark night-birds of the human heart shall one day give place to the birds of the morning, the sweet singers of the brighter day. *[Romans 15:13]* -J

380. How grateful we are O Lord that the drought of our ingratitude does not wither the green leaf of Thy sympathy and many undeserved kindnesses to us. *[1 Thessalonians 5:16-18]* -J

381. Great God, make our seasons of darkness to be opportunities for the unveiling of the Divine Presence. *[Ezekiel 24:18]* -J

382. Lord, we praise Thee for Thy sweet grace amid all the sudden and saddening upheavals of our intensely varied life. *[Ezekiel 24:18]*   -J

383. Blessed Master, grant to us a sound mind which delights in and passionately enjoys things that are pure. *[Philippians 4:8]*   -J

384. Father, help us to be like Jesus, neither frightened by the stones of the world, nor allured by its crowns. *[2 Timothy 1:7]*   -J

385. O God, cause our affections to become more and more sensitive, responsive, and vibrant to the griefs of others. *[John 11:35]*   -J

386. We are grateful Lord that Thy Word teaches us that true seekers shall be finders, and shall come into the satisfying presence of the unveiled glory. *[Jeremiah 29:13]*   -J

387. We praise Thee, Lord, that contemplation brings transformation. *[John 17:24; 2 Corinthians 3:18 (AMP)]* -J

388. Cause us, Lord, to gaze much upon Christ's glory and thus be utterly unconscious of ourselves. May we lose ourselves in Thee O God! *[John 17:24; 2 Corinthians 3:18 (AMP)]*   -J

389. Holy Spirit, teach us that if we are to enter into the joy of the Lord, we too must become people of sorrows and acquainted with grief. *[Isaiah 53:3; John 15:11]*   -P

390. Teach us O Lord that our mind can become a nest of petty purposes, when it was intended to be the glorious tabernacle of the eternal God. *[2 Corinthians 10:5]* -J

391. Lord, grant us to have a mind with large outlooks, which gazes upon big possibilities, and by the wideness of its gaze, sets things in their true perspective, and thus delivers us from the preoccupation with the trivialities of the passing day. *[Hebrews 12:1-2]* -J

392. Teach us, Lord, that our eating has a direct relation to the quality of our spiritual organism, and to be negligent about the one is to seriously impair and imperil the other. *[1 Corinthians 10:31]* -J

393. Lord, we know by sad experience that the flesh can be a heavy rider restraining the soul from its flights. *[1 Corinthians 10:31]* -J

394. Father, we praise Thee that at times You put resplendent treasures into commonplace earthen vessels in order that we may not think more of the vessel than we do of the treasure it contains. *[2 Corinthians 4:7]* -J

395. Most Holy God, unveil Thy love to us, so that in its clear shining we may behold the sin in our rebellion, and may turn unto Thee in humility and fervent devotion. *[John 17:23]* -J

396. Lord, impart to us the grace of simplicity. May our worship be perfectly candid and sincere. *[2 Corinthians 3:18]* -J

397. Father, quicken our perception that we may realize the Presence and feel the awe of the unseen. *[2 Corinthians 4:18]*   -J

398. Teach us O Lord that praise is an invincible armor—that we sing our way to the triumph we seek! *[Psalm 150]*   -J

399. We thank Thee Father for giving us the secret of conquest! "We are more than conquerors through Christ that loved us." It is conquest through the energy of an imparted love. Nay, it is much more than that. It is conquest through humble yet intimate communion with the Eternal Lover. *[Romans 8:37]*   -J

400. Mercifully meet with those who have been stunned with sorrow.   -J

401. Remember all who are in grave perplexity, and graciously light Thy lamp on their bewildered way.   -J

402. Receive all little ones into the circle of Thy blessing.   -J

403. Lead us into new fields of our wonderful inheritance in Christ.   -J

404. May some revelations of Thy love break upon our astonished vision.   -J

405. Help us to remember what we ought not to forget, and to forget what we ought not to remember.   -J

406. Let the beams of heavenly light chase out all the darkness of error.   -J

407. May the circles of our compassion grow larger every day.   -J

408. Let the ends of the earth be at our own doors, and so may we hear the distant cry.   -J

409. Make us missionaries of Thy truth and ambassadors of Thy grace and love.   -J

410. May we be quick to discern opportunity, and ready to use it in the service of our King.   -J

411. Help us to discern Thy footprints in the ordinary road.
                                                     -J

412. May the good desires within us be so strengthened as to destroy every desire that is vain.   -J

413. Make us mighty in consecration that we might be gracious in consolation.   -J

414. Help us to see Thy name on blessings that we never before recognized.   -J

415. Make us praiseful where we have been indifferent.
                                                     -J

416. Redeem us from our spiritual sloth.   -J

417. Eternal God, purify our souls and make our eyes keen and watchful in order that we may discern Thy purpose at every turning of the way.   -J

418. May His Gospel of grace become more exceedingly precious as we gaze into its unsearchable wealth.   -J

419. Let in the light as our eyes are able to bear it.   -J

420. Increase our faith that we may be led into the deeper secrets of Thy truth.   -J

421. Wilt Thou graciously grant unto us new possibilities of service?   -J

422. May we light lamps on many a dark road.   -J

423. May we give cups of refreshment to those who are thirsty.   -J

424. May our own faith and hope restore the flickering light where courage is nearly spent.   -J

425. Let us abide in quiet repose under the tutelage of the Holy Spirit.   -J

426. Inspire afresh in us Kindly Spirit, the ardor of enthusiasm that Thou alone can create.   -J

427. Thou Ever-Present Guide, bring us back into the clear path of Thy choosing.   -J

428. Rekindle the fire of our affections, purify the light of our conscience.   -J

429. Broaden our compassions and make them more delicate in their discernments.   -J

430. Impart unto us the saving sense of Thy companionship. -J

431. Almighty God, Our Father, may Thy presence ever give us companionship Divine. -J

432. Holy Father, unveil to us our poverty so that we may seek Thy wealth. -J

433. May we drink deeply at the waters of promise and thus find refreshment and strength in immediate duty. -J

434. Help us to gather up the needs of others in common intercession. -J

435. Quicken our imaginations in order that we may enter more deeply into the sorrows of Thy children in every land. -J

436. Steady our faith in these days of bewilderment. -J

437. In all the confusion of our day and age, may we never lose sight of Thy throne. -J

438. Let Thy Holy Spirit brood over us, quickening all that is full of promise, and destroying all that hinders our fellowship with Thee. -J

439. Eternal God, if we have been called upon to walk a weary road of unfamiliar sorrow, may we turn to Thee as to refreshing springs. -J

440. If we have missed a gracious opportunity, be Thou pleased to give us another chance.   -J

441. May we feel the burden of the burdened and weep with them that weep.   -J

442. We praise Thee Our Father, that many interpreting minds act like the solar spectrum and help to display the wealthy contents in the pure white light of Gospel truth. *[Ephesians 4:11-12]*   -J

443. Lord, may we reverently bear one another's burdens and carry them in the arms of intercession.   -J

444. We beseech Thee to grant us O Lord Jesus, glimpses of Thy glory in so far as our spiritual eyes are able to bear them. *[John 1:14]*   -J

445. Lord, surprise us continually with new discoveries among the mysteries of Thy Truth. *[John 17:17]*   -J

446. Look with pity, O Lord, upon this world in this hour of desolation and woe!   -J

447. Enlarge our hearts to comprehend the multitude of sorrows, and may we share the sufferings of our Lord in sacrificial labors. *[Philippians 3:10]*   -J

448. Lord, grant us characters of regal serenity, transparent and reflecting the very image of Thee Lord. *[2 Corinthians 3:18 (NIV)]*   -J

449. Father, purify our hearts by the permeating heat of affectional enthusiasm and devotion. *[Matthew 5:8]*   -J

450. Lord, won't You grant to us Holy Spirit-inspired fervent enthusiasm that we might spend it for the cause of Thy Kingdom? *[Revelation 3:19]* -J

451. Thou Gentle Flame, give to us Thine own fire that we might be endowed with the power of magnificent initiative. *[Ephesians 5:18]* -J

452. Fashion us Lord Jesus into the strength and beauty of Thine own image. *[2 Corinthians 3:18 (AMP)]* -J

453. Lord, grant that Thy people might face their difficulties with such splendor of character that their very antagonisms become the dark background on which Thy glory can be more manifestly revealed. *[2 Timothy 2:3]* -FM

454. Sweet Holy Spirit, help us to realize that our prayers, obscure and nameless though we are, can give utterance to a Paul, when Thou art controlling our lives! *[Romans 8:26]* -J

455. Lord Jesus, how wondrous is the thought, that to each of us is entrusted the marvelous ministry of helping others to receive the energies of Divine grace, as we pray for and encourage one another daily. *[Hebrews 3:13; Romans 8:26]* -J

456. We praise Thee, Our Father, that prayer opens our lives to the workings of infinite grace. *[Romans 8:26]* -J

457. What an awesome and wonder-filled thought Our Father, that through faith in the Lord Jesus, believers

are made everything He is and given everything He has. *[John 17:20-23]*   -JFM

458.   Thou Living Word, enable us to ponder deeply that in Thy precious Word, made alive and precious to our hearts, by Thy Holy Spirit, there is a whole ocean of boundless grace and truth rolling shoreless there before us. *[Psalm 119]*   -ML

459.   We praise Thee Our Father that Thy grace lights the dark horizon with the victory of the ultimate glory.
                                                              -MG

460.   How thankful we are, O Lord, that our critical need unveils Thy grace. *[Philippians 4:19]*   -J

461.   Father, how we desperately and constantly need a sound sense of Thy love to us in Christ. *[John 17:23]*
                                                              -TM

462.   Lord Jesus, how we praise Thee that Thy grace does not just measure up to our sin, but it rises above it in overmastering grandeur. *[Romans 5:20]*   -J

463.   Almighty Father, how we thank Thee that when our souls catch a glimpse of the riches of His grace, the wonderful vision moves us to inevitable and immediate praise. *[Ephesians 1:7]*   -J

464.   We praise Thee Lord Jesus that Angel's food can be found on fields of apparent disaster.   -J

465.   Father, may the unsearchable riches of Christ fit themselves into every possible condition of human poverty and need. *[Ephesians 1:7-8]*   -J

466. Thou Invincible Triune God, how we praise Thee that Thy grace is Thy sovereign will and power coming to expression for the deliverance of Thine elect from the servitude of sin. *[Ephesians 2:10]*   -JM

467. How thankful we are Our Father, that grace is Thy grand, glorious, good will distributing its gifts to those who are enslaved and winter-bound. *[Ephesians 2:1,8]*   -MG

468. Grant us O Lord an abundant supply of exhilarating gratitude which springs from sacred joy. *[Jeremiah 15:16]*   -J

469. Holy Spirit, lead us into the secret places of the Most High, that we might behold the marvelous unveilings of infinite love. *[Psalm 91:1]*   -J

470. Lord Jesus, we desire often to go to Calvary, Thy academy of love, and reverently contemplate the unveilings of Thy redemptive grace.   -J

471. Teach us, Spirit of God, that love and reverence are not the uncertain products of chance, but the sure and stately product of thought—of steady pondering Thy precious Word. *[Psalm 39:3]*   -J

472. We praise Thee Lord that in the fervent atmosphere of sacrifice buried seeds of possibilities awake into life.
          -J

473. Grant us Lord Jesus the grace to retain the heart of a little child that we might weep with them that weep;

and be broken-hearted when people reject Thee. May it be Lord that in these ways, in our own small way, that we might enter into "the fellowship of Thy sufferings." *[Philippians 3:10; Romans 12:15]*   -A

474.   Lord Jesus, may Thy resurrection power flow into our dormant affections and place into our hearts something akin to the tender sympathies and exquisite graces of Thine own heart. *[Philippians 3:10; Romans 12:15]*   -J

475.   We praise Thee Lord that though truth at times seems to be a frail and fragile creature and all but buried, she shall one day reappear in invincible majesty and shall incontestably dominate and command the affairs of men. *[John 14:6; 17:17]*   -J

476.   Teach us Lord that life only becomes fruitful when it becomes sacrificial. *[Philippians 3:10]*   -J

477.   O Lord, may Thy people be characterized by sacrificial fervor and thus multiply themselves throughout the race.   -J

478.   Teach us Lord that the measure of the impressiveness of even a poem, is just the measure of the sacrifice of which it is the shrine. *[Philippians 3:10]*   -J

479.   Holy Spirit, may we learn at the feet of Jesus that our most cheerful, sacrificial giving will result in our most joyful, abundant receiving. *[Acts 20:35]*   -J

480.   Lord, teach us to look at difficulties as promises in the guise of tasks.   -J

481. Praise Thee Lord, that John Bunyan is still fertilizing the field of common life with energies of rich inspiration. *[Ephesians 4:11-12]*　　　　　　-J

482. We praise Thee, Loving Father, that affliction introduces us to sweet juices and sustaining manna. *[Psalm 119:70-71]*　　　　　　-J

483. Father, by Thy Holy Spirit, we desire to offer unspeakable praise for Jesus, Thy unspeakable gift! *[Romans 8:26; 2 Corinthians 9:15]*　　　　　　-C

484. Lord Jesus, our longing desire is to praise Thee unspeakably for Thy unspeakable gift of Thy Holy Spirit to Thine own! *[John 17:22]*　　　　　　-C

485. Father, how we praise Thee for manifesting Thy glory in milder radiance, in the face of Jesus. *[2 Corinthians 4:6]*　　　　　　-S

486. Holy Father, our hearts overflow with thanksgiving and praise that You keep through Thine own name all those You have given to Christ. *[John 17:11]*　　　　　　-C

487. O Lord Jesus, when will we learn that Thy Holy Spirit cannot bless compromise!　　　　　　-S

488. We praise Thee Our Father, that, having received Christ, even a new, untaught believer will have in his new nature, a spiritual orientation bringing a desire for submission to Thy Word and Thy Holy Spirit.

　　　　　　-JFM

489. Tender Spirit, dwell with me, I myself would tender be. -J

490. Lord, grant to Thy people great hope that feeds the will, vivifies it and makes it steadfast and unmovable. *[Romans 15:13; 1 Corinthians 15:58]* -J

491. Lord, may our eyes be filled with the light of the heavenly vision even when we perform our earthly tasks. *[Colossians 3:2]* -J

492. Teach us Holy Spirit that walking with the Holy One, our elevation is our safety. *[1 John 1:7]* -J

493. We praise Thee O Lord, that truth, like its Maker, challenges our wonder the more we contemplate it. -T

494. Lord, how it thrills our hearts to find that the wonder of Christ is the wonder that does not vanish when it knows, but grows and deepens with everything it knows. *[John 17:3; Romans 11:33]* -GM

495. Lord, we long to be diligent doers and not merely casual hearers of Thy infallible Word! *[James 1:22]* -C

496. Lord, how we praise Thee that light floods into the dark cellar of doubt through the window of Thy precious Word! *[1 Peter 1:23]* -S

497. Teach us Thou Spirit of God that when we are all aglow with love to Jesus we find little need for amusement. *[Ephesians 5:16; 1 Thessalonians 5:16-18]* -S

498. Grant us Lord a church of out-and-out believers, impervious to soul-destroying doubt. *[Hebrews 11:6]*

-S

499. Teach us O Lord that we are only blessed that others we might bless! *[Hebrews 3:13; 10:24]* -JP

500. Perfect us in our intense desire and love for holiness and gradually complete its fulfillment. -JP

501. Thy love to us O Lord is our continual astonishment! May our reply to Thy love be a glad consent. -JP

502. Help us ever to read time in the light of eternity. -JP

503. May we see things on earth through the light of heaven. -JP

504. Lord, help our unbelief, transform it into triumphant faith. *[Mark 9:24]* -JP

505. To my heart daily be pleased to whisper Thy words of love. -JP

506. Thy Word is old as Thine own eternity, new as our present need. -JP

507. O Lord Jesus, Thou art the only answer to our sin, the only consolation of our sorrow. -JP

508. We bless Thee for every assurance of the existence of Thy throne. -JP

509. Enable us to hear all good voices and answer them gladly and gratefully. -JP

510. Lord hear us and astonish us with great replies! -JP

511. O Lord, Thy love to us is marvelous beyond all imagining. We will need the cloudless light of eternity to read the entirety of its beneficent purpose.
-JP

512. Praise Thee Lord Jesus for washing our lowly prayers and unworthy service and imparting to them royal value. -JP

513. Lord Jesus, cleanse all that we say and do that it may carry with it something of the atmosphere and grandeur of eternity. -JP

514. Lord, whisper some gentle word which shall cause singing in our hearts when no other voice can reach our weariness or heal our woe. -JP

515. Lord, help us to sense a more delightful and vital fellowship with Thyself. -JP

516. Father, ever create in us an irrepressible and holy desire for Thee. -JP

517. Help us to fix our wandering vision upon the abiding realities. -JP

518. Praise Thee Lord that though our sight leads us to despair, through our faith Thou dost send us gospels pure as dew, radiant as light, glad as music. -JP

519. Lord, save us from thoughtlessness. Help us to study one another with the anxiety of love. *[Hebrews 10:24]*
-JP

520. We bless Thee for a gospel so many sided. It is like a thousand doors opening upon the heart of God.   -JP

521. Undertake for us when our strength is gone and our sorrow is intolerable.   -JP

522. Lord, often grant to us a blessed consciousness of Thy Divine nearness.   -JP

523. May we rest our little griefs upon the infinite sorrow of the Son of God.   -JP

524. Lord, grant that we might become so saturated with Thy Word that it shall become to us safety and protection—invincible in every circumstance of life. *[Colossians 3:16; Ephesians 6:17]*   -JP

525. Lord Jesus, help us to ascend to Thee, our High Rock, that we might catch the light and inspiration of heaven.   -JP

526. O Lord, increase our gratitude. May the rain of Thy love not be lost in the desert of our insensibility. -JP

527. May the strength we derive from Thee Sweet Holy Spirit be expended in self-sacrificial, heroic imitation of the dying, rising, glorious Son of God.   -JP

528. Lord Jesus, may the royalty of Thy strength and grace rule our hearts with a sweet and welcome compulsion.
    -JP

529. O God, when the pulpit is wrong, how can the pew be right?   -JP

530. Father, grant us faith unshakable, that behind all the mystery of providence lies Thy purposes of love—vast as infinity. -JP

531. Father, cause our daily lives to be characterized by a more wakeful vigilance! -JP

532. May we hide ourselves in the sanctuary of Thy love. -JP

533. Lord Jesus, how we long to be with Thee where You are, where no hour of the endless duration shall be unblessed by the hallowed excitement occasioned by increasing intelligence and deepening love for Thee. *[John 17:24]* -JP

534. Father, we praise Thee for Jesus, the seal of Thy grace, the gift of Thy love. *[2 Corinthians 9:15]* -JP

535. Help us Sweet Holy Spirit to receive that bit of sunlight You would be pleased to grant us, that we might throw it back in generous reflection upon those who most need its help. -JP

536. Lord, pour psalms and hymns and spiritual songs into our hearts and graciously hear us when we sing them to Thee. -JP

537. Lord Jesus, be born in the Bethlehem of our spirits. -JP

538. Direct us in all perplexity by Thine unslumbering eye. *[Psalm 32:8]* -JP

539. May our whole life be tuned to the music of Thy Will.
-JP

540. Thou Triune God, by showing us Thyself, make the universe look small and make our life a throb of Thine own eternity. -JP

541. Lord, unsettle the foundations of every iniquitous throne. -JP

542. May we set our affections upon things above, and by a mightier gravitation than that of earth be drawn towards the throne that is established forever. -JP

543. We praise Thee Our Father for the sweet name of Jesus—crucified once, crowned for evermore! -JP

544. Lord, cause our souls to seek Thee, find Thee and hold long and sweet communion with Thee in all the speechlessness of enraptured love. *[1 John 1:3-4]* -JP

545. Almighty Father, tenderly make the bed of affliction, soften the pillow of pain. Often refresh us exceedingly upon our earthly pilgrimage. -JP

546. At Thy good pleasure Lord, let Thy Word flame like the sun, descend like the dew, or breathe into our hearts as the still small voice. -JP

547. Fill us with Thy sweet spirit of redeeming pity. We praise Thee Lord that where the background is blackest, every beam of Thy light shines with new and meaningful, dazzling brilliance. -JP

548. Just as the hen broods on her egg till life comes forth, so may we patiently ponder Thy Word till it becomes wonderfully alive and precious, bringing intense joy to our minds and hearts. *[Psalm 39:3; Colossians 3:16]*
-C

549. Whether our days be many or few, may they be bright with Thy presence. -JP

550. We muse upon the Son of God in Holy wonder; and as we muse the fire burns, and by its glow we know He is near Who is the light of heaven. *[Psalm 39:3; Colossians 3:16]* -JP

551. Remain with us Lord Jesus, yea, tarry with us lingeringly; and in that lingering we shall see Thy pledge of eternal fellowship. *[1 John 1:3-4]* -JP

552. Tender, loving Father, ever provide that wondrous balance; give us comfort in all sorrow, and chastening in highest ecstasy. -JP

553. Lord Jesus, we long to behold the light of that glad day when all Thine enemies are made Thy footstool.
-JP

554. O Righteous Father, grant to each of Thy children a sweeter consent to Thy Holy Will! -JP

555. Holy Father, enable us to see with greater clarity, that in Christ the highest solemnity is consistent with the purest joy. *[John 17:13]* -JP

556. Lord, may our heart be a hand, infinite in its ability to grasp the holy treasure received from Thy all-powerful hand of love. -JP

557. God of Love, create in us an agony of desire and grace to receive all the fullness of Thyself with which You would have us to be filled, according to Thy Divine timetable. *[Ephesians 3:14-21]* -JP

558. May we know that we are called to breathe the fresh air that comes from the hills of heaven. -JP

559. Show us that every loss is but an aspect of some great gain. -JP

560. Father, by Thy Holy Spirit, open our eyes that we may behold wondrous things in the Son of Thy love! -JP

561. Lord, help us to hate sin with infinite and unquenchable hatred! -JP

562. O Sun of Righteousness, help us to shed forth in holy reflection, Thine own brightness. *[2 Corinthians 3:18 (NIV)]* -JP

563. Lord, forbid that our knowledge of Thy precious truths should exceed our longing desire to impart them to others. -JP

564. O Thou Tender, Loving Creator, wilt Thou not provide for Thine own creatures, for that helpless, hopeless, starving multitude—not only food for their famished

bodies, but the Bread of Life for their immortal souls.
-C

565. Throw before our wondering vision the things that are not seen and eternal, and fill us with a holy desire to be for ever with Thee. *[John 17:24; 2 Corinthians 3:18 (AMP)]* -JP

566. Lord Jesus, we know that Thou art there by the flooding love which overflows our being. *[John 14:21]* -JP

567. Lord, wean us from the fascinations of time and sense. *[2 Corinthians 4:18]* -JP

568. Lord Jesus, come to us with answers larger than our prayers, and with revelations that shall astound our vision by their beauty and magnificence. -JP

569. Soothe grief too sensitive to be approached by the kindest human love. -JP

570. When the night is long, teach us to charm away all its darkness by continual songs of hope. *[Romans 15:13]* -JP

571. Father, Thy words to us are like music to our hearts because they come to us tender with the tremulousness of Thine own love. -JP

572. Almighty Father, in Thy giving we saw Thy whole heart—all the love of Thine eternity, and all the grace of Thine infinitude. *[John 3:16]* -JP

573. Send light upon lives that have slipped down into caverns of great darkness. *[John 8:12]* -JP

574. May our whole life rise up to Thee like a temple towards the heavens, complete and beautiful and resonant with Thy praise. -JP

575. Great Triune God, let the helplessness of the weak be the reason of Thy coming to them in the almightiness of Thy grace. -JP

576. Sovereign of the universe, our longing desire is to enter into the innermost place of Thy dwelling, there to behold such of Thy glory as our vision can endure. *[Psalm 91:1; John 17:24; 2 Corinthians 3:18 (AMP)]* -JP

577. Our desire is to love Thee more understandingly! -JP

578. Enter into every one of our houses, not as a glance of light, but as an abiding glory. -JP

579. Lord, enable us to find the bridge of Thine own building over every difficult river. -JP

580. Father, may we be in spiritual vision as quick to discern Thy Divine Presence as we are to see the disadvantages of life. -JP

581. O Our Father, we confess that our faith needs constant strengthening. The more we believe, the more we also want to cry out with the father of the boy with the unclean spirit, "I do believe; help my unbelief." *[Luke 17:5; Mark 9:24]* -JFM

582. We praise Thee Lord that the cemeteries of Thy people become, through the heavenly dew, the resurrection fields of the promised perfection. *[1 Corinthians 15:49]*   -JFM

583. O Lord Jesus, since You were *despised and rejected of men*, may we not seek to be highly *esteemed and respected of them*. *[Isaiah 53:3]*   -P

584. O Thou Savior and Lord, we praise Thee for saving us from the slavery of sin, that we might be wholeheartedly, though very imperfectly, obedient to Thee out of very gratitude and love to Thee, our God and Master, our All in All! *[Romans 6:17]*   -C

585. O Lord Jesus, we grieve when men reject Thee; we suffer when Thy people fail to respond to the pleadings of Thy very own Word—to strive to be like Thee (1 Jn. 2:6), to quote Scripture in temptation (Mt. 4:4; Eph. 6:17); and to let Thy Word dwell in them richly (Col. 3:16) so that out of the abundance of their heart their mouth would indeed speak (Mt. 12:34)! O Lord, could this be fellowship with Thy sufferings (Phil. 3:10)? *[1 John 2:6; Matthew 4:4; 12:34; Ephesians 6:17; Colossians 3:16; Philippians 3:10; Hebrews 3:13; 10:24]*   -C

586. O Father, grant to us as Thine own a sweet reasonableness and Holy Spirit sensitivity that we might, out of very love to Thee, fervently pray for one another, and, in pleading love, seek to spur one another on to our very best for the cause of Christ and

the upbuilding of Thy Kingdom. *[Philippians 4:5; Hebrews 3:13; 10:24; James 5:16]* -C

587. O Lord Jesus, repeatedly press us into Thy precious Gospel mold that Thy image might more clearly be stamped upon us. *[Romans 6:17 (NAS)]* -C

588. Father, may we in very deed be among those who rejoice evermore, and pray earnestly without ceasing! *[1 Thessalonians 5:16-17; James 5:16]* -C

Prayer to Receive Christ

"Lord Jesus, as best I know how, I am coming to You, admitting that I am a lost sinner, and asking You to come into my life and save me and change me, and make me the kind of person You want me to be.

"Give me the grace (or ability) to trust You and You alone, Lord Jesus, for this salvation and the change You bring. In Your name I pray, Lord Jesus, Amen."

Breath-Heartbeat Prayer

(To Receive Christ)[2]

"Lord Jesus, if there is any chance that I am not now saved, let every breath that I breathe, and every heartbeat that my heart beats, call upon You, asking You to come into my life and save me and change me, and make me the kind of person You want me to be. Give me the grace (or ability) to trust You and You alone, Lord Jesus, from this moment on, for this salvation and the change You bring. In Your name I pray, Lord Jesus, Amen."

---

2.   For those who lack assurance of salvation.

Appendix A[1]

God's Terms of Salvation

"If any man would be saved, he must believe that Jesus Christ is both *Lord* and *God*. Again, you must confess that Jesus Christ is *Lord*, that is, *Ruler* and *Master*. You must cheerfully become His disciple, follower, and servant. You must confess, 'He is my *Master*; He is my *Lord*. I intend to be a soldier under Him. He shall be to me *Leader* and *Commander*; God has made Him such, and I accept Him as such.' You are vocally to own Jesus; you are definitely and distinctly to say with your tongue, your mouth, your lips, that he is your *Lord* and *Saviour*.... With my mouth I do again confess the Lord Jesus, for I believe Him to be *very God of very God*, my *Master*, My *All*."

—C.H. Spurgeon

"Your lying professions mock Him.... If you have never believed in Him and repented of sin, and yielded obedience to His command, if you do not own Him in your daily life to be both *Lord* and *King*, I charge you lay down the profession which is so dishonouring to Him. If He be God, serve Him; if He be *King*, obey Him; if He be neither, then do not profess

---

1. Except as noted, quotes extracted from *Quoting Spurgeon*, Baker Book House, 1994 (Used by permission).

to be Christians. Be honest and bring no crown if you do not accept Him as *King*."

—C.H. Spurgeon,
A Treasury of Spurgeon on the Life and Work of Our Lord,
Vol. 6, p. 410 [Matthew 27:29]

"Submission to the will of God, to Christ's lordship, and to the guiding of the Spirit is an essential, not an optional, part of *saving faith*. A new, untaught believer will understand little of the full implications of such obedience, but the spiritual orientation of his new nature in Christ will bring a desire for submission to God's Word and God's Spirit. A person who does not have that *desire* has no legitimate claim on *salvation*."

—John F. MacArthur, Jr.

"The baby *sucks*, instinctively; and the born-again person also feels a hunger for spiritual food—first the milk and then the meat of God's revealed Word (1 Peter 2:2; Hebrews 5:12-14; 1 Corinthians 3:2). He listens to the Word preached and taught and discussed; he reads it in his Bible; he asks questions about it; he meditates on it, memorizes it, chews the cud on it, labours to squeeze all the goodness out of it. 'Oh, how I love Thy law! It is my meditation all the day…. How sweet are Thy words to my taste, sweeter than honey to my mouth!' (Psalm 119:97,103). Constantly to crave for God's Word and to want to go deeper into it is thus a second sign of being regenerate…Regeneration is no more (and no less!) than the work of God in our hearts *which leads to the gospel being whole-heartedly received.*[2] If only God would make us simple enough to see this and, having seen it, never to lose sight of it! Then the Christian world would be a very different place.''

—J.I. Packer

2.   Romans 6:17.

Appendix B

**Prayers Compiler Pleads With Fellow
Christians to Make a Part of
Their Daily Private Prayer Life:**

When you wake in the morning pray:

"Father, render me dead to sin.[1] Cleanse me by the blood of Jesus.[2] Fill me with Thy Holy Spirit[3] and lead me by Thy Holy Spirit[4] this day and all the days of my life. Likewise, may this prayer apply to all of Thy people. In Jesus name I pray—Amen"[5]

"Father, give me the grace right now to consider myself dead indeed unto sin[6] but alive unto Thee through Jesus Christ my Lord. Shout in the ear of Satan that You sent the Lord Jesus Christ to expose Satan and all the demons to be shattered, empty and defeated in Jesus' own triumphant victory at the cross where he shed His precious blood for the sin of the world.[7]

---

1.   Romans 6:11.
2.   1 John 1:7.
3.   Ephesians 5:18-19; Colossians 3:16.
4.   Romans 8:14.
5.   Compiler's Note: This is a paraphrase of a prayer Dr. D. James Kennedy recommended several years ago that I have made a part of my daily prayer life.
6.   Romans 6:11.
7.   Colossians 2:15 (*Phillips*).

"Give us eyes to see the excellencies of Jesus, and then to exchange all that we are for all that Christ is![8]

"Further, Our Father, may my roots and the roots of all Thine own go down deep into the soil of Thy marvelous love[9] and may the power of Thy Holy Spirit working through us accomplish infinitely more than we could ever ask or imagine.[10] In Jesus name I pray, Amen."

---

8. Psalm 84:9.
9. Ephesians 3:17.
10. Ephesians 3:20.

Appendix C

There is a real consensus among the great pastor-teachers that these are the five most marvelous prayers in all of Scripture. The editor pleads with all Christians to consider making these a part of their daily private prayer life!

"Oh, my brethren, you will not do better than to quote Scripture, especially in prayer. There are no prayers so good as those that are full of the Word Of God."

—C. H. Spurgeon

John 17:17-26

17 Sanctify them through Thy truth: Thy word is truth.

18 As Thou hast sent Me into the world, even so have I also sent them into the world.

19 And for their sakes I sanctify Myself, that they also might be sanctified through the truth.

20 Neither pray I for these alone, but for them also which shall believe on Me through their word;

21 That they all may be one; as Thou, Father, *art* in Me, and I in Thee, that they also may be one in Us: that the world may believe that Thou hast sent Me.

22 And the glory which Thou gavest Me I have given them; that they may be one, even as We are one:

23 I in them, and Thou in Me, that they may be made perfect in one; and that the world may know that Thou hast sent Me, and hast loved them, as Thou hast loved Me.

24 Father, I will that they also, whom Thou hast given Me, be with Me where I am; that they may behold My

glory, which Thou hast given Me: for thou lovedst Me before the foundation of the world.

25 O righteous Father, the world hath not known Thee: but I have known Thee, and these have known that Thou hast sent Me.

26 And I have declared unto them Thy name, and will declare *it*: that the love wherewith Thou hast loved Me may be in them, and I in them.

Ephesians 3:14-21

14 For this cause I bow my knees unto the Father of our Lord Jesus Christ,

15 Of whom the whole family in heaven and earth is named,

16 That He would grant you, according to the riches of His glory, to be strengthened with might by His Spirit in the inner man;

17 That Christ may dwell in your hearts by faith; that ye, being rooted and grounded in love,

18 May be able to comprehend with all saints what *is* the breadth, and length, and depth, and height;

19 And to know the love of Christ, which passeth knowledge, that ye might be filled with all the fulness of God.

20 Now unto Him that is able to do exceeding abundantly above all that we ask or think, according to the power that worketh in us,

21 Unto Him *be* glory in the church by Christ Jesus throughout all ages, world without end. Amen.

Ephesians 1:15-23

15 Wherefore I also, after I heard of your faith in the Lord Jesus, and love unto all the saints,

16 Cease not to give thanks for you, making mention of you in my prayers;

17 That the God of our Lord Jesus Christ, the Father of glory, may give unto you the spirit of wisdom and revelation in the knowledge of Him:

18 The eyes of your understanding being enlightened; that ye may know what is the hope of His calling, and what the riches of the glory of His inheritance in the saints,

19 And what *is* the exceeding greatness of His power to us-ward who believe, according to the working of His mighty power,

20 Which He wrought in Christ, when He raised Him from the dead, and set *Him* at His own right hand in the heavenly *places*,

21 Far above all principality, and power, and might, and dominion, and every name that is named, not only in this world, but also in that which is to come:

22 And hath put all *things* under His feet, and gave Him *to be* the head over all *things* to the church,

23 Which is His body, the fulness of Him that filleth all in all.

Philippians 1:8-11

8 For God is my witness, how greatly I long after you all in [the affection and tender mercies of Christ Jesus Himself].

9 And this I pray, that your love may abound yet more and more in knowledge and *in* all judgment;

10 That ye may approve things that are excellent; that ye may be sincere and without offense till the day of Christ;

11 Being filled with the fruits of righteousness, which are by Jesus Christ, unto the glory and praise of God.

Colossians 1:9-12

9 For this cause we also, since the day we heard *it*, do not cease to pray for you, and to desire that ye might be filled with the knowledge of his will in all wisdom and spiritual understanding;

10 That ye might walk worthy of the Lord unto all pleasing, being fruitful in every good work, and increasing in the knowledge of God;

11 Strengthened with all might, according to His glorious power, unto all patience and longsuffering with joyfulness;

12 Giving thanks unto the Father, which hath made us fit to be partakers of the inheritance of the saints in light.

Topical Index

Scriptural Index

Prayeraphrases® was developed
from the following authors and sources:

Author	Author Code
Charles H. Spurgeon (approx. 33%)	S
John H. Jowett	J
Alexander MacLaren	ML
Joseph Parker	JP
The Compiler	C
F.B. Meyer	FM
G.H. Morrison	GM
John F. MacArthur, Jr.	JFM
G.C. Morgan	MG
D.M. Lloyd-Jones	LJ
A.W. Tozer	T
Thomas Manton	TM
Joseph Alleine	A
A.W. Pink	P
John Murray	JM
Count Zinzendorf	Z
Thomas Watson	TW
Andrew Murray	AM
Marcus Rainsford	MR
George Burrowes	GB
Walter E. Bowie	WB
E. Schuyler English	E
W. Graham Scroggie	WS